LITTLE GIANT

I0555366

"A refreshing break from typical success stories...this beautiful book is a fountain of inspiration about living adventurously and on your own terms."

—William Parkhurst, *New York Times* bestselling author of *True Detectives*

"*Little Giant* offers wisdom on business and friendship from an improbable venture on the Caribbean island of Aruba."

—Murray Carpenter, author of *Caffeinated* and *Sweet and Deadly*

"I wish there were more books like this. It's the beautiful story of two men chasing their dreams—not in the default 'more is better' way but in their own unique way. It was also inspiring to feel the author's own transformation happening throughout the book...it reminded me of *Tuesdays with Morrie*. The design, structure, and flow of the book was original and refreshing."

—Paul Millerd, author of *The Pathless Path* and *Good Work*

"This book sounds like a great feel-good movie, something cooked up in Hollywood. Well, the 'feel good' is certainly there, but the story is very real. This book is for the dreamers in all of us."

—BookTrib

"This is a very human book about choices and what can happen when people truly love each other. It depicts a different way of life and doing business, where you can have your cake and eat it, too. It's full of inspiration, humor, and wisdom."

—Mickey Green, award-winning filmmaker

"The characters and their stories moved and delighted me, and the book itself is gorgeous."

—Shelley Sperry, author of *What's the Big Idea?*

"The author weaves together moving interviews of the two cofounders with fascinating quotes from artists, philosophers, and psychologists. The result is an inspiring guide to composing a meaningful life."

—Betsey Feeley, former coordinator of the Literature Award Program at the American Academy of Arts and Letters

"This compelling exploration solves the mystery of how to thrive through intense difficult waves. The inquisitive author interweaves oral histories as well as psychological studies to enliven our understanding of our own dreams, life, and work."

—Elizabeth Garber, author of *Sailing at the Edge of Disaster*

"I love that David and Yair knew what their 'enough' was... they wanted to create something that served the community and made an enjoyable life for them and their wives. They didn't want to raise capital, build fast, and take it public or sell it to a bigger company. They kept it small, and in doing so show us all a different path."

—Glen Van Peski, author of *Take Less. Do More.: Surprising Life Lessons in Generosity, Gratitude, and Curiosity from an Ultralight Backpacker*

Little Giant
The Story of Aruba's Surf Shop and the Rebels Who Built It

Marcia Heath

 L'il Nob Press

Little Giant: The Story of Aruba's Surf Shop and the
Rebels Who Built It

Copyright © 2024 by Marcia Heath. All rights reserved.
No part of this book may be used or reproduced in any
manner whatsoever without written permission except
in the case of brief quotations in the context of critical
articles or reviews.

ISBN: 979-8-9897206-0-6 (paperback)
ISBN: 979-8-9897206-2-0 (ebook)
ISBN: 979-8-9897206-1-3 (hardcover)

Cover design by Laura Duffy Design
Book design by Adam Hay Studio, UK

To protect the privacy of certain people profiled in this
book, some names and identifying characteristics have
been changed. All the people interviewed for the book
graciously gave their permission to quote them.

Printed in the United States of America

https://littlegiantbook.com

CONTENTS

For Matt Weed

You amaze and inspire me.

Aruba
Dutch Caribbean

2.5 Hours to Miami

Wreck California

California Dunes

California Lighthouse

Druif Beach

Unknown Wreck 17th Century

Warizuri

Arashi Beach

Wreck Antilla

Malmok Beach

Fisherman's Huts

Alta Vista Chapel

Ritz Carlton

NOORD

Wreck Debbie

Palm Beach

Boardwalk Boutique Hotel

Bubali Bird Sanctuary

Ayo Rock

Wreck Rumrunner

Casibari F Formati

Eagle Beach

PARADERA

Hooiberg

Manchebo Beach

Bula ARUBA

ORANJESTAD

SANTA CRUZ

Cruise Ship Terminal

Queen Beatrix International Airport

Wreck Tugboat

Barcadera

Wreck Jane (

Wreck Old Mi Dushi

N

E

W

S

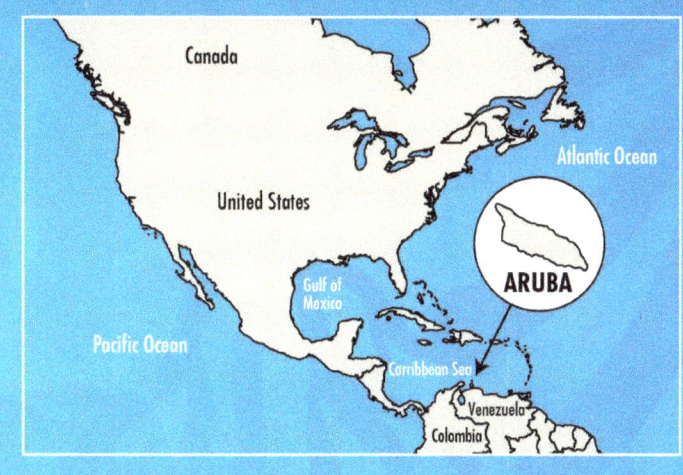

Canada

United States

Atlantic Ocean

ARUBA

Pacific Ocean

Gulf of
Mexico

Carribbean Sea

Venezuela

Colombia

Wreck French Bark

l Bridge

on

Boca Keto
Natural Pool

Dos Playa

Arikok
Natural Park

Frenchman's Pass

Spanish Lagoon

Savaneta

r Island

Santo Largo

Wreck Galleon

Boca Grandi

SAN NICOLAS

Rodgers Beach

Baby Beach

Wreck Captain Roger

CARIBBEAN SEA

The Book I Wrote After I Lost My Mind, Left a Perfectly Good Job, and Sat Under a Mango Tree

My husband came home and found me wandering from room to room in a wool skirt and a bathing-suit top. I kept insisting I was late for work. It was a balmy summer day, a Saturday. I'd lost my mind, quite literally. David took me by my arm and drove me straight to the emergency room.

Hours later, I woke up, groggy and disoriented, in a cramped cubicle. My vitals blinked on a glowing green monitor. I wondered, *What am I doing here?* David handed me a packet of crackers and patted my arm as the ER doctor fired questions at me.

"Who's the president of the United States?"

I came up blank, then made a wild guess. "Hillary Clinton?" The doctor looked vaguely amused.

"What year is it?" he asked.

I had no clue. (It was 2017.)

"Where do you live?"

"Boston." I hadn't lived in Boston for decades.

After an MRI and a battery of other tests, a soft-spoken neurologist delivered the diagnosis. I had a relatively rare case of transient global amnesia (TGA), a sudden episode of short-lived forgetting most common in people between fifty and seventy. The chief symptom of TGA is anterograde amnesia, or the failure to form and hold new memories. Asking the same questions, over and over, is a telltale sign: *Where are you taking me? What's happening? Why am I here?* People with TGA lose the ability to make new memories or retrieve old ones, though they know their own names and can walk, speak, and follow instructions.

The eclipse of memory typically lasts four to six hours. Mine lingered longer. I had to stay overnight in the hospital for observation. It was a surreal experience. I slept, had weird dreams, and woke up sobbing, completely untethered. The next morning, it was as if someone had flipped a switch. My body and mind reconnected, and the memories flooded back. Most of them. Except for a few stray impressions, my brain erased the memory file of what had happened during the TGA episode itself.

Neurologists consider TGA a "benevolent syndrome" with no long-term effects. Researchers can't tell us how a TGA occurs, but they can point to severe emotional distress as a common trigger. That was my situation. The morning of the TGA, I woke up with heart palpitations and a terrible headache. I hadn't slept. I couldn't shut off the worries about my job. Which was odd, because I'd just gotten a promotion. My new office overlooked a neighborhood park. I could ride my bike to work. The gig seemed just about perfect.

The consulting firm prided itself on being a creative, fun place to work. But the more I pushed myself to fit into the rah-rah culture, the more powerless and phonier I felt. I'll never forget the day that Joe, my new post-promotion boss, handed me a plastic Halloween mask. We were sitting next to each other at an employee event.

"You can win the rat race, but you're still a rat."

BANKSY, ENGLISH GRAFFITI ARTIST
AND FILM DIRECTOR

"Show your team spirit," he commanded. Much as it sickened me, I slipped on that dumb mask and grimaced as the elastic band tightened around my skull. As the weeks ticked by, Joe became more aggressive and controlling. At erratic intervals, he'd storm into my office and bark military-style commands at the bookcase behind my desk. It was risky to ask a question. Questions made him raise his voice and speak more slowly, as if explaining string theory to a child or an elder. Mid-sentence, he'd pivot and leave. As soon as the door slammed shut behind him, I'd grab the bottle of Excedrin I kept in my desk drawer. If need be, I swallowed the tablets without water; a trip to the kitchen wasn't worth the risk of an encounter with Joe.

Every day I dragged myself to the office, and every day I fantasized about quitting. But quitting was for losers, right? I felt like a wimp in executive clothing, with no escape in sight. I pinged from project to project with a whack-a-mole velocity, a rat in a labyrinth. I had turned into a one-trick wonder, churning out copy on tight deadlines. When I left the office at night, I sometimes forgot to push the down button in the elevator. I'd just stand there, catatonic. I was so tired, so worn down, I could feel the weight of my eyelids when I blinked. The thing is, I hardly recognized myself. I looked normal, but I was all hollowed out inside.

As scary as the TGA episode was, it gave me the existential jolt I needed to see the futility of my work situation. My brain and body rebelled at a time of crippling stress. After I got out of the hospital, I put my finances in order, talked things over with David, and asked myself a simple question: If I could do one thing, right now, to better my life, what would it be?

The answer was gratifying and clear. Officially, I resigned for health reasons. The company president, Megan, took me out for a farewell meal. As soon as the breadbasket landed on the table, she pressed me for the details on my resignation. I fended off her questions as I ordered pasta primavera in honor of my new beginning. Was it cowardly to say nothing about Joe? Probably. But I had no fight left in me. I just wanted out. No more white-collar purgatory for me.

A few months after I left, the grapevine buzzed with news about Joe's abrupt departure from the company. By then, in mid-2017, I had set myself up as a freelancer working out of a makeshift office in the guest bedroom. At first the transition felt awkward, like walking through first-class to an economy seat, but the personal freedom thrilled me.

I retired my alarm clock, got hooked on Russian Caravan tea, and took up gig rowing. The freelance projects trickled in, a mix of ghostwriting, strategic planning for start-ups, and copywriting for ad agencies. After the honeymoon period ended, though, I couldn't shake the question: *Was this the best I could do?* I felt like a sellout, coasting on the fumes of past accomplishments. Creatively, the work left me cold.

As a kid I had absorbed the message that creative writing and other forms of personal expression didn't count for much. They certainly didn't qualify as gainful employment options. So, over the years, I tamped down the dream of telling my own stories, in my own voice, and on my own terms. At the core, I harbored nagging fears I would expose myself as a pretender, a faux talent. When you add in my talent for procrastination, you have a serious case of creative paralysis.

It's odd my breakthrough moment came from a couple of Aruban surf-shop owners, but that's exactly what happened. Their courageous choices intrigued me so much, I refused to waste any more of my limited life span waiting for the right moment to push my limits as a writer.

> *"You can't count on success; you can only leave open the possibility for it, and be ready to jump on and take the ride when it comes to you."*[1]
>
> AUSTIN KLEON, ARTIST, AUTHOR

Lose your mind. Leave a perfectly good job. Drift along as a freelancer. Yes, it's a strange way to introduce a story about living the good life in the Caribbean. As it happens, the heroes of this book suffered their own versions of a career meltdown, not unlike my own. In their late twenties, they found themselves locked into a life path that made them miserable.

All over the world, and in many different ways, untold numbers of people get caught in a similar bind. Many of us live split-screen lives: the ones we lead and the alternative lives of our dreams. Maybe we have the talent and intelligence to follow a passion, but we deplete our energy obsessing over our options or chastise ourselves for dreaming. Maybe we sleep too much or too little. We're too worried, distracted, or self-effacing.

Often it takes a crisis to shake us free.

In the early days of Covid, almost exactly three years after I quit my last office job, I developed a thirst for a more creative, fulfilling life. Like millions of others, I felt isolated from my friends and existentially adrift. When my freelance projects dried up, I started reading books, lots of books, about the pursuit of happiness. I steeped myself in the latest social science research and ventured into other fields, including neuroscience, Stoicism, and creativity studies.

As a lifelong over-complicator, I was constantly taking my temperature. *Am I happy? Am I happy enough? What is a good life anyway? Maybe I should take up Tai Chi . . . eat more blueberries . . . learn Portuguese . . . give up caffeine . . . plant an organic vegetable garden.* I had turned into one of those confused, self-absorbed characters you see in Woody Allen movies.

One morning, buttering my toast, a paradoxical thought caught me by surprise: *Can trying to be happy make you unhappy?* This was my truth, sad to say. My studious pursuit of happiness had only succeeded in sucking me dry. Although I didn't realize it at the time, my experience wasn't all that unusual. Obsessive self-focus can undermine our happiness, the research tells us. We're happier when we direct our energies elsewhere—on meaningful projects, ideas, and people outside our immediate realm of experience.

> ## *"Those only are happy who have their minds fixed on some object other than their own happiness."*
>
> PHILOSOPHER JOHN STUART MILL

As a diversion, I picked up a copy of *Travel + Leisure* magazine. My eyes landed on a photo of a beautiful couple on recliners at the edge of an emerald sea. They gazed outward, toward a distant horizon, as a bright orange sun slid into the sea. I remember chuckling to myself about how obvious it was: I needed a rejuvenating break from Maine's gray skies, and Aruba was an ideal getaway. My husband's son (also named David) lived there with his wife, Debbie. Luckily, we could stay in their guest apartment.

David and Debbie had moved to Aruba in early 2003. Over the years, my husband and I visited them a handful of times. We always made a ceremonial visit to Bula, the surf shop David owns with his best friend, Yair (pronounced *yah-eer*). It was a welcoming kind of place, even for a nonsurfer like me, and I could always count on Yair to help me pick out a cool new pair of sunglasses.

When the authorities lifted the Covid ban on travel, David and I boarded a plane to Aruba. The first afternoon, I plopped down next to my stepson on the outdoor sectional in his small urban backyard. He had just returned from a day working at Bula, and we chatted in the dappled shade of an Alfonso mango tree, one of fourteen exotic varieties he'd planted. David had to wait several years before his trees bore fruit. Now his backyard was a garden of ripening mangoes of all sizes, some as large as a kid's football.

That afternoon, Aruba's famous trade winds tugged at my clothes and made my hair fly. All the branches shook and the leaves rattled. It was so noisy, I slid closer to David to catch his words. He casually mentioned he'd made it a habit to go surfing every day during the pandemic closures.

"Without all the tourists, the beaches were empty and really beautiful," he told me. "I would have enjoyed it more if I hadn't been so worried about the world ending."

With one of the most tourism-dependent economies in the Caribbean, Aruba had been gutted by the pandemic. The Royal Plaza Mall, Bula's home base, had turned into a ghost town overrun with vacancy signs and shuttered storefronts.

David surfed his way through the pandemic.

"So how's Bula doing?" I asked, bracing myself for bad news.

"Actually, things are pretty great." He put his feet up on the teak coffee table, bleached white by the Aruban sun. "Bula's fine, and Yair and I are still having fun." His answer intrigued me. Fun? Doing great? It struck me that David and Yair might be years ahead of the curve in refusing to follow the rise-and-grind culture. Maybe they could teach me, an anxiety-prone overachiever, a few things about living with greater ease and enjoyment.

With quiet pride, David told me about Bula's 2021 holiday season. Customers had waited in long lines stretched out the door and around the corner. Even with extra staff, they could barely handle the crowds.

"Christmas is always our busiest time," David explained. "It's been like that ever since we opened." I quickly did the math: This was Bula's eighteenth Christmas marathon, a rare feat of survival. Entrepreneurs live and breathe risk. First-time founders like David and Yair face an 82 percent rate of failure.[2] Most start-ups go out of business in a year or two, and only 30 percent of the remaining few make it past the ten-year mark.[3]

By the numbers, Bula qualifies as a freak success. Against the odds, David and Yair had turned their passion for ocean sports into a hugely popular and profitable business. They weren't superheroes, more like mild-mannered Clark Kents. But when the opportunity presented itself, they put on the cape, took the leap, and propelled Bula toward a thriving future.

It took me two years of sleuthing to piece together the clues to Bula's unlikely success. You will learn how David and Yair overcame enormous obstacles and survived on grassroots support that never wavered. Many of their decisions were ahead of the times, starting with their decision to put friendship above money, status, and prestige.

Instinctively, they had grasped what I'd learned from reading the social science research on happiness. People with a strong network of friends are happier, healthier, and live longer. Lonely people suffer disproportionately from illnesses, both physical and psychological, and die earlier.[4]

Loneliness is a warning signal,
as grave a risk to our health as smoking
fifteen cigarettes a day.[5]

David Putnam (center) and Yair Lichtenstein (right) outside the shop.

Relying on their trusty buddy system, David and Yair built a community-based business the locals flocked to from Day One. Neither of them ever cracked a single self-help book or marketing tome. This was a revelation for me, a self-improvement junkie. I had other blind spots, too—about surfing culture, retailers, and the inner workings of male friendships. Surprise: Surf shops aren't overrun with hygiene-challenged stoners.

Little Giant began as my love letter to David, Yair, and the many kind, inspiring people I met on the island. They taught me so much about my own dreams and helped me fulfill an elusive one—writing this book, my first. I'm solid proof it's never too late in life for a reboot, a fresh start, or a major recalibration.

By the time I finished the project, I realized that what I'd written might also inspire anyone who's ever dreamed of taking a bold leap but never quite made it happen. So whether you are ready for a change right now or dreaming of a different future, this book dares you to hit the reset button and pursue whatever has been knocking at the door of your heart.

Freedom Seekers

On April 7, 2003, David Putnam and Yair Lichtenstein swung open the doors of Bula Surf Shop in Aruba's capital city, Oranjestad. Their love of ocean sports had inspired them to start an authentic surf shop, run for and by surfers. Yair, a native Aruban, chose a perfect name for their fledgling venture. In Papiamento, Aruba's local language, *bula* means "to jump" or "to fly."

As idealistic young cofounders, they took a flying leap into uncharted territory. Both jettisoned their careers to gamble their life savings on a hidden-away surf shop. They weren't your typical entrepreneurs with MBAs or special business training. Neither had a day of retail experience, let alone a clue about the realities of running a small business in Aruba.

Bula Surf Shop started as a tropical adventure, a lifestyle experiment, and a full-on rejection of establishment culture. Essentially, David and Yair fired their employers, saying "Thanks, but we'll do things our own way now." They wanted to be their own bosses, rewrite the rules of work, and spend their time on projects of their own choosing.

Pre-Bula, David had earned a law degree and had a good running start on a career in the satellite communications field. With his graduate degree in marine science, Yair had landed a coveted assignment as a field researcher in the Galápagos Islands. Every day, he got to walk in Darwin's footsteps and ponder how to save the world's oceans. Everything was humming right along for them both, and not just professionally. Each had recently fallen in love with new girlfriends. All the external markers of success were locked, loaded, and ready to spring.

Or so it seemed.

After a couple of years, their original career choices closed in around them like a trap. For a few months, they floundered in career limbo. Then, one day, they put their heads together and made a pact: *Let's, together, ditch the routine and follow a dream.* When they announced their plan to open a friendship-based surf shop, their friends in traditional careers feared they were headed straight off a cliff without parachutes. Because really, how much fulfillment could two ambitious young men expect from selling surfboards and T-shirts?

Once David and Yair jumped the rails, they never looked back. I suspect each of them had a bit of a subversive streak, wanting to prove the doubters wrong. Unlike many youthful entrepreneurs, David and Yair didn't set out with grandiose plans to start a revolution, scale the business, or make millions by a certain date. They simply wanted to earn enough money to live comfortably while spreading their passion for ocean sports out into the community. As they made their leap, they gave themselves three unusual rules to live by:

- Stay best friends, no matter what.

- Do something good for the local community.

- Have fun.

Bula grew from quiet roots, with a minimum of fanfare. There was no razzle-dazzle launch party or PR blitz on opening day. David and Yair showed up at the shop with sand between their toes and salt in their hair. They'd marked the occasion by heading out at dawn for a ceremonial surf off the wild north coast of Aruba. Their unorthodox experiment had officially begun.

What David and Yair did is something millions of us dream of doing. They made a courageous decision and acted. All of us have to make life-altering choices: Where should we live? Whom should we marry? How will we earn a living? Trouble is, most of us don't have a good sense of what will make us happy. I know I didn't. For more than two decades, I zigzagged along on a path in communications—a perfectly sensible choice for an English Literature major with publishing aspirations. I got to travel internationally and work on interesting projects. As a brand strategist, I developed a knack for promoting the talents of other people. But I was pretty terrible at recognizing my own worth and abilities as a writer.

This bugged me at a deep, cellular level, but not enough to take action. I stayed stuck for the longest time. Then there was that serendipitous moment I mentioned in the Preface. Talking with David under the mango tree, something happened I can't explain. An inner voice calmly told me: *You've got to chase this story*. For once I didn't second-guess myself to death. I just knew, deep in my bones, that I would follow the trail of the Bula adventure, wherever it took me.

When I first told David and Yair about my book idea, they didn't exactly jump for joy. They can't have been thrilled by the prospect of putting their lives under a microscope. David and Yair are two of the most private—and humble—people I've ever met. They quickly pointed out that they never had a ten-point plan or magic formula. Especially in the first few years, they made quite a few boneheaded moves, operated on naive assumptions, and acted out of an excess of idealism.

But there's no denying their remarkable achievements as cofounders. Bula bears a striking resemblance to a Purple Cow, a term coined by the best-selling author and business guru Seth Godin. Purple Cows are innovative companies of all sizes that flout formulas and get noticed because they're counterintuitive and exciting. Every day, consumers overlook a lot of brown cows, Godin writes, but they never ignore a Purple Cow. In Aruba, Bula's a Purple Cow. You can't ignore it. And you don't want to, because it's an exciting place.

David and Yair eventually agreed to the book as long as I kept a promise: *No claiming.* Claiming is a gesture a beginner surfer, a kook, might make after a good ride. A claim is equivalent to a fist pump in tennis or an end-zone dance in football. In the surfing world, hardcore surfers frown on claiming. It's considered showy and embarrassing—definitely not cool.

In observance of the no-claiming rule, you'll read about topics you might never expect in a follow-your-bliss tale: clinical depression, surfing injuries, inventory debacles, hungover employees, and peevish customers. David and Yair fought an unending series of troubles, and as bootstrappers of a small business, they made some whopper (and often hilarious) rookie mistakes.

I just love how they sum up their success: "We went from stupid to less stupid."

As much as possible, I told the story in David and Yair's own words, as informal oral histories. During the many months of interviews, they found their natural groove as narrators. Both of them excelled as wisecrackers and self-deprecating raconteurs. Never once did they boast about their obvious successes, so I had to do some of that for them.

Be forewarned, *Little Giant* breaks the mold of a typical business biography. You won't find a neatly packaged blueprint for brand building (though Bula is a kick-ass brand) or the "10 secrets" of an innovative start-up. The narrative rolls along with a single mystery at its core: How do you turn a passion into something tangible and fulfilling? Woven throughout you will find a smattering of inspirational quotes and a running commentary on David and Yair's every wipeout and each wave of success.

I spent a lifetime waiting for the discipline and maturity to write this book. That I've now written it is proof of neither of these things, but it does attest to the spirit of adventure David and Yair so freely shared with me.

ACT I

1

The First Two
Hundred Hours

On the first day of the January semester in 1994, Yair Lichtenstein strode into the Art 101 classroom at the University of Miami. He carried a greasy waxed-paper bag oozing with guava pastries. He'd picked them up, freshly baked, at a nearby Cuban cafe. Yair loved the intense sweetness of the guava paste mingled with the thick cream-cheese filling. All his life, he'd been an enthusiastic eater. Yair could out-eat anyone at any table, but he never put on an extra pound.

With his thick dark hair and scruffy beard, Yair had a brawny handsome look. He came dressed for class in shorts, flip-flops, and a pink T with the words *Sailboard Vacations Aruba* across the front. He loved that shirt so much. Every time he wore it, strangers would come up to him and gush about the beaches in Aruba or its near-perfect sunny weather.

Yair scanned the classroom and chose a seat next to a student with curly brown hair. David Putnam had a face full of freckles and a tan from a recent visit with his father in Key West. They'd caught a boatload of mutton snapper and went lobster diving. David loved anything to do with the ocean. As the child of divorced parents, he had lived primarily with his mom in Charlotte, North Carolina. His adventure-seeking father (my husband) often planned expeditions that took them far and wide—usually into water or trouble of some kind. They caught river trout in Montana, threw cast nets in Sarasota, and dove for lobsters and conchs in the Bahamas.

Like many native Arubans, Yair took up windsurfing at a young age. In his early twenties, he became a fanatical surfer, an obsession that fueled his dream of opening a surf shop.

Like Yair, David was on the skinny side, scrappy, and inquisitive. He picked up skills with lightning speed. And also like Yair, David had put on his favorite clothes for the first day of class: a faded blue Polo shirt and quick-drying shorts frayed at the hem.

David got early lessons in shrimping from his father, an avid outdoors expert and on-air talent for a CBS affiliate in Miami, Florida.

Neither David nor Yair were particularly arty, but both needed to check off a humanities requirement. David was on the honors track, rounding out his major in international politics and a minor in Japanese. Yair hoped Art 101 would lighten his load of classes in oceanography, marine biology, and chemistry.

As Yair settled into his seat, David introduced himself and pointed to Yair's T-shirt, asking the obvious question: Had he ever been to Aruba?

"Yeah, that's where I'm from. I'm Yair, by the way."

"Hey, I went to boarding school with a guy from Aruba, Russ Reynolds." David paused. "I know it's kinda weird, but do you know him?"

"Sure, kind of." Yair took a pastry out of the bag.

Russ had been a minor bully and a renowned jackass at David's boarding school in Pennsylvania. David couldn't stand the guy, and he felt a little tightening in his gut just thinking about him.

"Was Russ a friend of yours?"

"No way, he was such a douchebag." Yair looked at David and smiled. "Want a guava pastry?"

Right then, David knew Yair was an A-OK guy. Not only did he know a douchebag when he saw one, he was polite enough to share his breakfast. David took a bite of the pastry and looked around the room.

Just then a student sitting right behind them accused another student of looking at his girlfriend in a lustful way. At first, David and Yair thought the guy was kidding. Then the jealous boyfriend started jabbing his trigger finger at a tall rangy student with heavy stubble.

David and Yair couldn't believe the boyfriend's paranoia.

"If you look at her one more time," he shouted, "I'll break all your fucking fingers."

The accused student mumbled something and shrank down in his seat. His face flashed crimson red. David and Yair shot him a sympathetic look as the professor walked into the room. They whispered comments about the boyfriend's outburst—and kept it up for the rest of the class.

"We'd just witnessed this really random example of toxic masculinity," David told me during one of our interviews. "It was weird watching this guy with bad social skills getting aggressive."

"Yeah, we replayed the scene for a few days," Yair added. "We'd laugh, you know . . . it bonded us as friends because we saw the absurdity in the situation the exact same way."

The classroom incident sparked a lifelong friendship spent laughing at oddball situations. Whenever David and Yair ran into something especially bizarre, they'd relive the high points and tease out the humor. They kept the riff going, watering it like a houseplant. Their special brand of friendship grew naturally from the garden-variety seeds of connection—pizza, movies, sports—and a lot more horsing around and laughter.

Yair's blunt honesty in calling a mutual acquaintance a douchebag may seem minor, but how often do we censor ourselves, especially in unfamiliar social situations? We don't want to offend, so we hide our true reactions. Although they had just met, Yair and David instinctively trusted each other. They traded quips the same way kids trade baseball cards. Their humor meshed, and ultimately, so did their friendship.

The psychologist and friendship expert Robin Dunbar has developed a fun predictor of who will become good friends. He calls it the Seven Pillars of Friendship:[6]

1. Speak the same language or dialect.
2. Share the same educational experience and/or career (notoriously, medical people flock together, and lawyers do the same).
3. Share the same world view (a combination of moral, spiritual, and political views).
4. Have the same sense of humor.
5. Grow up in the same geography.
6. Have the same hobbies and interests.
7. Like the same types of music.

The more of these boxes you tick off with someone, the more emotionally close you become. I'm no psychologist, but I'm confident David and Yair met the criteria for the first four pillars right away. We all tend to gravitate toward people with whom we have a lot in common. We like people who are most like us. The birds-of-a-feather syndrome—it's called *homophily*—holds true. Just as pigeons flap around with other pigeons and crows with crows, humans tend to hang with other humans with similar traits. Except that we're also complex creatures. Often we don't know why we're drawn to some people and not others. And sometimes our dissimilarities add spice and depth to our friendships.

Such is the case with David and Yair, though they didn't know this at the time they met. They just knew they liked each other and felt comfortable in each other's company. Their conversation had a natural and effortless flow. They instinctively recognized they were from the same tribe.

I discovered in our continuing interviews that they had something else in common. They were both lonely.

Yair and David immediately bonded as fellow
outcasts in their Art 101 college class.

"It Was a Little Weird How Easy It Was."

Yair: I met David soon after I transferred to the University of Miami from the University of North Carolina at Chapel Hill. I knew my roommate, and that was about it. My academic adviser had recommended Art 101 to knock off a humanities requirement. As soon as I walked in, I noticed a bunch of football players, frat boys, and miscreants messing around. I knew I wouldn't get along with anyone else in the class. Then I saw David, and I took the seat next to him.

David: I was in my second year when I met Yair. I wasn't desperately lonely or anything. I had made some friends. But I definitely didn't fit in with the heavy jock-party scene the campus was known for. I took the art class hoping I'd meet some interesting arty types. But I saw right away the class was full of people with zero artistic talent, and I included myself in that category. I remember sitting there, wondering what I'd gotten myself into, when Yair sat down.

Yair:	David was a really good conversationalist. Right away we got talking.
David:	It was a little weird how easy it was. We made fun of everyone else, but really, we were the weirdos in that class.
Yair:	Right! The first week we met, I remember seeing a poster about an Alvin Ailey modern jazz dance performance. Now, I'm definitely not into dance, but it seemed like something an aspiring college intellectual might want to do. David immediately said, "Yeah, I'll go." It was a sign. I guess we were signaling we had the same artistic proclivities.
David:	I was totally up for it.
Yair:	I remember we both pretended we had fun, but I'm quite sure we were bored to tears.
David:	Yeah, sounds about right.

David and Yair became permanent, fast friends within a few months. It was almost as if they had no choice in the matter.

"Yeah, it wasn't as if we made some big conscious effort," Yair explained. "When you're really good friends, you *want* to keep in touch. Maybe you discover a good record and want to share it with that person because you know they'd like it. Or you meet this girl. It's exciting, so you tell your friend about her."

Family dynamics may help explain why they clicked on many different levels. David was an only child. Yair took the role of the brother David never had. And Yair wasn't particularly close to his own brother, who was six years older. David slipped into that role for him, his super-close brother by choice, not genetics.

Neither recalls ever "working at" becoming friends.

"That's the strange thing," David told me. "When you're with a great friend, you don't question it. There's an alchemy. I don't know how else to say it."

Still, none of us can just snap our fingers and make a friend. Friendships don't just drop out of the sky. A famous study found it takes roughly fifty hours of accumulated time to move from a mere acquaintance to a casual friend. To establish a true friend—someone who accepts us at our worst and rescues us in a crisis—it typically takes more than two hundred hours.[7]

On a college break, they went fishing in the Dry Tortugas, 70 miles south of Key West. David caught a nice tarpon that day.

The lesson here: The two-hundred-plus-hours rule isn't a sacred formula. We don't need to clock our friendship hours as if we're counting calories. The bonding process is largely unconscious, exactly as Yair said. We're psychologically wired to put in time getting to know people, and the effort doesn't have to deplete us. Mundane meetups count, especially if they're face-to-face.

So how did David and Yair fill up their first two hundred hours? Between classes, they went out for Cuban coffee and crispy-fried pastries. Sometimes they'd grab a burger at the Rathskeller, the university's student-run restaurant. On weekends, they might go with a group of friends to a band concert or dance at a club at South Beach. The Miami club scene wasn't really their thing, though. They have the fond memories of driving in David's clunker Suburban, listening to music and smoking weed. They also remember spending long evenings with their inner circle of friends, pretending they were going to go out later that night but never actually leaving the dorm room. It was standard college fare: spontaneous, relaxed, practically on autopilot.

All that changed when David decided to spend his junior year studying in Tokyo. Now they had to figure out how to keep their friendship intact while separated by a gulf of 7,454 miles.

Off-Road Adventures

David and Yair explored the shores of Iceland as one of their many college excursions. When David spent his junior year in Tokyo, they met up for trips to Indonesia, Singapore, and Malaysia. They also joined a group of friends on a quintessential $10-a-day backpack trip through Europe. After a few days, they split off from the herd after slumming it in bed-bug-ridden hostels with iffy toilets. They didn't see the point of pretending to be impoverished when, for a few extra dollars, they could sleep in comfortable beds. A budget-but-comfortable style suited them both: no to sleeping bags, yes to functional indoor plumbing. As fellow travelers, interested in off-the-beaten-path experiences, they rarely disagreed about anything. Their easygoing compatibility boded well for their future joint retail venture.

2

So Many Forks
in the Road

The day David left Miami and moved to Japan for a year, the friendship with Yair hit a crossroads. Any long-distance relationship constitutes a struggle, and theirs was no exception. They had to make a conscious choice to stay best friends. Or not.

"I got a little nostalgic on the flight to Tokyo," David told me. "All my life I'd been a pretty independent Type A, but I definitely felt a little homesick leaving Yair and other friends of mine behind."

This was the mid-1990s: pre-internet, pre–social media, pre–cell phones. David and Yair didn't have WhatsApp or FaceTime video calls at their fingertips. Racking up hundreds of dollars in long-distance phone calls wasn't a practical option either. Instead, David and Yair sent each other aerograms. The foldable, light-blue letters now seem as quaint as quill pens; back then, they were a popular, inexpensive form of communication. David and Yair went to creative lengths to use all the space, including writing extra small, filling the margins, and using arrows and diagrams.

The two friends stayed connected, despite the distance and trouble. It's a little odd, really, to think of two college buddies making their friendship such a priority. Unless things go terribly wrong, friendship isn't a subject most of us obsess over, certainly not with the fervor of our romantic relationships. As a practical matter, friendships are vague and voluntary, easily sliding into the background of life. And unlike marriage or parent–child relationships, friendships aren't bound by legalities or a commonly held set of societal expectations.

Experts often refer to friends as our "family of choice." It's so true. Lovers may come and go, but our best friends stay, sticking with us through good times and bad. That was essentially what David was getting at when he said, "When you find someone you really get along with and enjoy spending time with, you just don't ever want to give that up."

Like millions of other recent grads, David and Yair faced a rocky entry into the real world after college in the mid-1990s. It was a time of testing for both of them. They'd spent the previous few years acing the roles of professional students. With their degrees in hand, they faced the usual irksome questions: Who am I? What are the important things in life? What are my options for the path ahead, and how do I even make a path?

Most colleges don't teach classes on path-making for young adults. For many of us, the path to pinning down a viable career can feel about as clear as the plot of a *Choose Your Own Adventure* storybook, where readers choose their own endings based on guesses and limited information. Inevitably, we each absorb random pieces of advice along the way about what society expects of young adults of our ilk—which is weird, because "society" knows so little about us. At least career counselors give us a battery of tests before steering us toward safe careers. But too often, they're jobs we can't ever imagine ourselves doing. And then there's the hovering presence of our concerned parents.

In the famous 1967 movie *The Graduate*, a young Dustin Hoffman plays Benjamin Braddock. He's fresh out of college, idly floating in his parents' pool, when his father, played by William Daniels, accosts him.

William Daniels: What are you doing?

Dustin Hoffman: Well, I would say that I'm drifting here in the pool.

William Daniels: Have you thought about graduate school?

Dustin Hoffman: No.

William Daniels: Would you mind telling me then what those four years of college were for? What was the point of all that hard work?

Dustin Hoffman: You got me.

Haven't we all at some point felt that way? Just drifting through life (though not necessarily in a luxurious pool). The discomfort can strike during any major transition: when we leave college and enter the workplace;

question our next move in mid-career; or stress over retirement. After David graduated with top honors from the University of Miami, I knew he had faced a similar crisis of indecision, and I asked him to tell me about it during one of our interviews.

"I thought about going back to Japan," he said. "I liked living there, but liking Japan was hardly a viable career. I allowed myself to be persuaded by dear old Dad, who suggested I go to law school. He pitched it as a launchpad for whatever career I might eventually choose."

Of course, neither David nor his father had an inkling he would end up running a surf shop in a constituent country of the Netherlands.

Ironically, a law professor poisoned David on pursuing a legal career. Raj Bhala, a professor of International Trade Law at George Washington University, walked up to the chalkboard one day in class and plotted out the standard life trajectory of a high-paid lawyer: entry into prestigious law firm, crushing workload, commute, children, mortgage, mega salary, mansion in the 'burbs.

Professor Bhala meant it as a cautionary tale about setting good life priorities, but the scenario sounded unbelievably grim to David. He had already decided he didn't want kids, and he wasn't particularly motivated by the lure of a fat paycheck or a fleet of Mercedes in the garage.

Not long after Bhala's lecture, David picked up a magazine at a local bookshop near the law school campus. Skimming the table of contents, he zeroed in on a new research report about the most and least rewarding careers. Roofers, dentists, and lawyers scored abysmally low on the satisfaction scale. The findings fit his own private assessment. The more he learned about law, the less he liked it. Still, dropping out of law school wasn't a path he seriously considered.

David felt tremendous pressure to tough it out, especially from his socialite grandmother. During his occasional visits to Palm Beach, Florida, she paraded him around her exclusive social club, bragging about his future as a high-powered attorney. As David said, "She had a clear image of me as a partner in an elite law firm, wearing custom suits in a big office with an ocean view."

David soldiered on and earned a law degree. Soon afterward, he took a rogue detour, much to the dismay of his grandmother. Even his supportive father worried that his brilliant, hardworking son had slipped his moorings.

With his best friend from first grade, Greg Lucas, David hatched the idea for an innovative satellite communications start-up in D.C. The fledgling company quickly found its footing, and David thrived on the manic pace and autonomy. The start-up did so well that it was soon bought out by a larger telecommunications company. David and his partner signed a contract to stay on during the transition to the new owners.

The year was 2001. David was twenty-seven years old and already established as a rising entrepreneur. He loved making his own seat-of-the-pants decisions. Post-buyout, he spent his days babysitting bureaucrats, pretending to pay attention in meetings, and dodging petty power plays. Most everything bugged him: the numbing paperwork, the rush-hour traffic, even the rattle of the coffee cart.

As David finished up his contractual obligations, he got a hastily scribbled postcard from Yair, who was in Aruba dealing with his own career crossroads. Post-college, Yair had suffered long dark stretches of anxiety about what would become of his life. On the day he'd fired off the postcard to David, Yair had just gotten back from surfing his favorite break on the north coast of Aruba. He had recently quit his job as a field researcher on the Galápagos Islands. His abrupt exit perplexed his mentor, Georgina Bustamante, one of the region's leading marine scientists. Dr. Bustamante had expected Yair to take the marine conservation field by storm. And so, privately, had he.

Unlike David, who had caved to parental pressure to give law school a try, Yair had made his own decision and felt sure he'd found his true calling as a marine scientist. After growing up fishing, diving, and windsurfing off the rocky coasts of Aruba, he'd imagined himself as a protector of the world's oceans. The Galápagos gig was a plum first assignment, a dream come true on the islands where Darwin did his pathbreaking research.

Almost right away, Yair got hit by nagging doubt. Instead of condemning the fishing community he had come to interview, he felt empathy. Yes, they were breaking the law and fishing unsustainably, but in Yair's mind, it came down to poor families just trying to survive as they had for centuries.

What could he do about it, really? Illegal fishing was a huge, messy problem of corruption on a global scale. He was just one smart-ass kid tasked with writing a condemning report. It all seemed so futile.

Yair's initial fervor slipped away.

As Yair wrote up the last interviews, he fell into a deep depression and had panic attacks. At times, even tying his shoelaces felt overwhelming. He struggled to complete his assignment and put words on the page. He was tempted to quit. Dr. Bustamante warned him that if he did, he would never again be hired in an academic or research position. She urged Yair to come up with a plausible excuse and take a break. He thanked her profusely and promised to think it over.

Yair packed up his research papers in a box and penned a contrite letter of resignation. Then he asked his parents if he could crash at their guest apartment, and, ever supportive, they welcomed him back home. He spent his days making big pieces of driftwood furniture with a chainsaw and surfing at Wariruri, a remote cove known for its treacherous currents. A friend trucked the heavy loads of waterlogged wood from Wariruri Cove to Yair's parents' house, and in no time, fanciful creations populated the backyard. Working with his hands gave Yair a reprieve from worrying about what he would do with the rest of his life.

In 2002, to an outsider, both David and Yair looked perfectly poised for a lifetime of success. High-status degrees: *Check*. Cool places to live: *Check*. Impressive resumes and credentials: *Check*. But the seeds of doubt had already started to germinate. Fortunately, they stayed in touch regularly by snail mail, phone, and the occasional in-person visit. They didn't let their friendship wither as so often happens after college, and that made all the difference when each of them reached a turning point and needed each other's support.

Why did they stay tethered instead of drifting apart like so many other ambitious twentysomethings? When I asked him to reflect back on that time, Yair didn't give me a glib answer.

"I suppose we'd just gotten in a self-perpetuating habit," he said. "Talking or writing to David always gave me a psychic boost, especially when things sucked."

The postcard Yair mailed David during his depressive phase came from a rack at a local beach shop, a tourist trap selling flip-flops, bikinis, and the occasional surfboard. The card featured a sandy beach at sunset lapped by the Caribbean Sea. On the back, Yair scribbled the first thing that came to mind— "Beach Til We Die"—and put the postcard in the mailbox without signing his name. He knew David would know who sent it.

Yair hit a low point in 2002 after he abruptly resigned from his research gig in the Galápagos and moved back home to Aruba.

Saved from "Dying Inside"

In 2002, David and his best childhood friend, Greg Lucas, took a celebratory drive in David's trusty Volvo after selling their satellite start-up to a government contractor.

David practically grew up at Greg's house, where they binged on Cheetos, swilled orange sodas, and played video games nonstop. David kept their largely unsupervised activities secret from his mother, who fed him a regimented vegan diet.

On the rare occasion when Greg hung out at David's house, he remembers eating "yucky food . . . brown rice and chickpeas" in the kitchen.

"We weren't allowed in the dining room," Greg told me, "because his mom turned it into a display room for all her crystals. She didn't want us to mess up the energy."

Much later, as business partners, Greg and David helped each other survive the year of transitioning the new owners of their company. They got along most of the time but occasionally broke into heated arguments under the stress.

"If you don't have radical transparency as business partners," Greg explained, "you'll never make it through the hard times." As trusted friends, they were able to build a successful business and amicably hash out any creative differences.

Greg credits David with saving him from "dying inside" a few years after the sale of their business. With David's encouragement, he quit a dead-end job and leapt into a dream career in the Asheville music scene. "I was more the wishy-washy dreamer," Greg told me. "David was the realist and strategist, the one with the seriously good ideas." Decades later, Greg admits he's still awed by David's ability to dissect a problem and come up with creative solutions.

3

The Gift of Desperation

Yair went through his morning ritual of making a giant thermos of black coffee, dosing himself. These days, it took a steady infusion of caffeine to jolt him awake. He'd brewed the coffee extra strong to get all his brain cells firing. As he puttered around his parents' kitchen, Yair mentally rehearsed what he wanted to say to David. His idea stood a slim chance of surviving the ultrarational David test. With his law school training, David would have made a great prosecutor, and Yair didn't relish being on the defense team.

In Bethesda, Maryland, David sat hunched over his desk in a windowless office painted the anonymous murky green of hospital waiting rooms. He remembered the phone ringing, the lilt of Yair's voice. His brain fog lifted as he imagined Yair in Aruba, surrounded by his woodworking tools and remnants of driftwood from his favorite surf break. David still couldn't quite believe Yair chainsawed all the odds and ends into fully functional furniture—a rustic sofa, side tables, a bench, and a variety of mismatched chairs.

"Hey, how are you?" Yair raised his voice so David could hear him over the din of Aruba's trade winds and settled into the stargazing chair he'd just finished.

"Still sucks." David leaned back in his chair. "I can't wait until this nightmare is over." His desk was overrun by three-ring binders and stacks of reports from the new corporate owners of his start-up.

"I'm sorry, man."

"What's the news from there?"

"I dunno, I'm driving my parents nuts." Yair glanced at the pile of driftwood in the backyard. "The chainsaw's so damn noisy, and they go to bed early."

"Got it. How's the surfing?" David knew Yair went surfing most days.

"Oh, that's great, except I snapped a board yesterday, and there's nowhere to go to get a new one on the Island."

"Really, I would have thought—"

Yair cut him off mid-sentence. "Yeah, I know. But that gave me an idea. Maybe we could open a surf shop, you know, an actual surf shop, run for and by surfers. Believe me, Aruba doesn't have any such thing, surprisingly enough."

David straightened in his chair. It was an insane thought. Tightening his grip on the phone, he let the idea percolate. His mind flashed back to the first time his father took him to Surf City Surf Shop in Wrightsville Beach, North Carolina, when he was eight or nine. As a skinny nonsurfer, David felt total awe for the buff surfers milling around in the shop. The shop's owner saw him lurking in a corner and took him on a tour of the skimboards. That surf shop was the coolest, most welcoming place David had ever been. He never forgot the floaty sensation of walking out with a fancy new skimboard under his arm.

Right away, David loved the idea of replicating that magical childhood experience in Aruba, but there were so many obvious strikes against Yair's idea. What did either of them know about retail? Nothing, except for random impressions of shopping in other people's stores. David had never visited Aruba. He couldn't imagine living permanently on an arid speck of volcanic rock within sight of Venezuela. He'd have to learn Dutch, Spanish, and Papiamento, the local dialect. And he could only guess at the hassles of getting a work permit as an American citizen.

Plus, he'd have to learn to surf. He couldn't own an authentic surf shop and not surf, could he? It had been difficult enough to find his balance on the skimboard. There was really no way in hell this idea of Yair's made rational sense.

"Hey, David, are you there?" Yair stood up and took a few steps toward the house, cradling the phone against his ear with his shoulder. It was blowing 23 knots, nothing unusual for a July day, but the gusts made it difficult to hear.

"Oh, sorry . . . that actually sounds . . . really good." David got up and paced around his office.

"No, really? Seriously?"

"Sure, that sounds awesome." David couldn't quite believe the words coming out of his mouth. "I want to get in on that."

That's really all it took—one phone call—to put an initial plan in motion. They were both so burnt out, the idea of doing something brazen and possibly foolhardy seemed just right. The two friends batted some ideas around for a few more minutes and came up with a first step: a scoping expedition to check out the competitive retail scene in Aruba.

At the end of the call, Yair told David he had a friendly name all picked out for their future shop: Bula. As a kid, Yair had dreamed of getting a boat for his birthday and naming it Bula.

His parents never gave him a boat. So then he dreamed of getting a dog and naming it Bula. That didn't happen either. As it turned out, the first—and last—thing he got to name Bula was the surf shop.

The forces of nature carved Wariruri, a sandy cove, out of coastal limestone along Aruba's north shore. Wariruri attracts hardcore surfers and fishermen, who fish along the low cliffs framing the cove on both sides. Photo credit: wheninaruba.com

After his call with David, Yair's heart thumped at double speed—and not just because of the caffeine. He shoved a board into the back of his truck and bumped along the rutted roads leading to Wariruri Cove. With the radio cranked high and the windows open to the wind, he tapped his fingers on the steering wheel in time with the music.

When he arrived at his usual spot, Yair found a clean swell underlying the usual choppy windblown Aruban conditions. Yair got in a few good rides, popping to his feet and connecting turns on the wave face. Reading the incoming waves required a deep meditative focus, a total immersion in the moment.

As any surf expert will tell you, you have to "look where you want to go." In surfing, you need to stay focused on the wave as it reels ahead of you. If you look at your feet, as beginners often do, you invariably regret it. You activate downward muscle movements that can throw you off balance. As you lose your balance, you panic, aggravating the problem.

Looking down—instead of ahead at your goal—nearly always guarantees a wipeout.

For Yair, surfing that day at Wariruri, it was all about living in the moment, looking toward the horizon. No second guessing. In the same spirit, when David and Yair went to the edge and took their communal leap of faith, they never once looked down.

"Do What You Need to Do to Be Happy."

Yair: Who knows what I was thinking back then? It was more than twenty years ago. I had gone to grad school to become a marine scientist. When I outgrew that, so quickly, my ego took a hit. It was confusing: *Hey, this was what I was supposed to do.* Pragmatically, though, I knew I was unhappy. It was time to do something different. A mental breakdown will do that for you—it gives you that clarity.

David: Yair had a genuine existential crisis. My situation was different. I was miserable, serving out my time, but at least my buyout contract had an end date. The question for me was: What's next? I always knew I could practice law, maybe in Japan. I didn't have a problem with being a lawyer, not really. A law degree is useful in many ways. But what stayed with me was what Raj Bhala said that day. I totally got the idea that law school students had privileges—a certain IQ, economic background, social networks. These advantages are tools that *should* buy us freedom. So why stick with a law career if it makes you miserable?

Yair: Yeah, really good points. My graduate school mentor, Georgina, said something similar. She's a supersmart marine biologist, but also a very interesting human being. She escaped from Cuba on a raft that was adrift for days. When I quit the job in the Galápagos, she told me it was a really bad career move. But if I needed to go back to Aruba and be with my family, she understood. "Do what you need to do to be happy," she told me. Georgina didn't buy into the idea that we're entitled to a single linear career path. That was a luxury in Cuba where she grew up. Of course, I didn't know at the time I'd open a surf shop. If she had known that, I wonder what she would have said. . . .

David: Yeah, I wonder what Raj would say if he knew he'd inspired one of his law students to throw everything away, move to the Caribbean, and start a surf shop. Maybe it would put a smile on his face. I hope so.

Where did David and Yair find the courage to end one chapter of their lives and start another? In the course of one phone conversation, they decided to risk their futures on a retail shop tucked away on the second floor of an aging mall. They had no financial backers or start-up funds in reserve. They were like a couple of kids daring each other to leap off a cliff into a lake. In unison, they ran to the edge and jumped. In this case, into the southern Caribbean Sea.

Most of us spend more time second-guessing our appliance choices than pondering what will make us happy. Analysis paralysis can keep us mired in indecision even when the choices aren't all that life changing. Psychologists say the root cause of analysis paralysis is anxiety. We fear choosing the wrong option. But something in David and Yair's mindset quieted their nerves and gave them the courage to jump.

No matter what happened, they had each other's backs. David and Yair had shared many of the same passions for years—water sports, beach life, and offbeat adventures. Their values and interests meshed on a deep level. It helped, too, that they were still young and figured they could recover, professionally, if Bula tanked as a business. And neither was tied down by marriage, mortgages, or children.

Paradoxically, it was lucky they had both suffered debilitating career setbacks at roughly the same time. Yair's dream career in marine science had sent him spiraling into a clinical depression. David's exposure to big business bureaucracy soured him on the prospect of working for anyone else again. In hindsight, they were handed the gift of desperation. Both craved something completely different—fun, adventure, independence. They had already proved to themselves they could succeed, at least for a short while, by society's standards. Now it was time to seek success on their own terms.

4

The Fallout

David had stalled as long as he could. For weeks he'd dreaded telling his grandparents his news. As the plane landed in Palm Beach, Florida, David tried to think of a way to make running a surf shop in the tropics sound like a promising career choice for someone with a law degree. His grandparents were already upset enough that he'd never taken the bar. Now, instead of imagining him in a fancy law office, they'd have to picture him folding T-shirts in a retail space squeezed between souvenir shops selling bikinis and sunscreen.

David hopped a cab from the airport to the Everglades Club, a bastion of old money in Palm Beach. His grandparents made their usual fuss, showing him off like a shiny new trophy to their social clique. Amidst all the cocktails and glad-handing before dinner, David didn't have a chance to drop the bombshell about his Aruba plans.

He took his assigned seat at a table set with sterling-silver candlesticks, a heavily starched tablecloth, and crisp napkins folded like flowers. His dinner companion was a socialite friend of his grandmother. Mrs. Harwood, a recent widow, wore a nubby pink suit and a helmet of perfectly coiffed silver hair. Through the multi-course meal, from the Waldorf salad to the after-dinner mints, she baited David with questions about law school, his girlfriend, and his job prospects. As the tedious meal wore on, David lowered his guard and dropped a couple of vague hints about moving to Aruba and starting a surf shop.

Unbeknownst to David, Mrs. Harwood was a notorious gossip. The next morning, at the earliest acceptable hour, she phoned David's grandmother.

"How wonderful that your darling grandson is opening a surf shop," Mrs. Harwood gushed. "You must be so proud."

It was country-club code for *how perfectly dreadful that your grandson is such a loser, you poor thing.*

David's grandmother slammed down the receiver and stormed into the guest bedroom where he was still asleep. She shook him awake and started talking faster and much louder than usual. He remembers her perched on an antique chair, trembling with rage.

"If you do this, never expect one thing from me," she hissed. "Not one cent."

She stormed out of the room, muttering. He'd never seen this scary side of his normally reserved grandmother. Her emotional outburst shook him so much he hid in the bedroom until he heard the crunch of her Lincoln Town Car tires rolling down the gravel driveway.

Growing up, David had spent a lot of time with his Florida grandparents. During visits to the exclusive Bath & Tennis Club with his grandmother, he darted around the pool like a tadpole and dove for quarters in the deep end. David would slip out of his swimming gear into a kid-sized sports coat, tie, and penny loafers for the obligatory dinners at the Everglades Club. On moonlit nights, the ceiling over the dance floor slid back to reveal a spectacle of palm trees. Couples danced to the mellow sounds of a live orchestra under starry skies. David worked hard not to fidget too much during the long, boring dinners with his grandparents. Even as a kid, he spotted the pretension.

The contrast of David's life with his mother in Charlotte and those Palm Beach visits must have felt surreal. His mom studied arcane aspects of astrology and embraced vegan practices long before they entered the cultural mainstream. She enforced strict rules for what David ate (organic), how he dressed (only natural fibers), and even things as esoteric as the direction of his bed (a certain compass point). The New Age lifestyle so dismayed her parents that they had axed her almost completely out of their lives. Now, just as David was about to start a new business in the tropics, his maternal grandparents turned their backs on him, too—financially and in every other way.

"That's how unimpressive they thought I was," David shared with me. "My grandmother made it clear I was a total social embarrassment to her and her snooty friends."

Just like that, David found himself estranged from his disapproving grandparents and truly on his own in the world. If things got really desperate, he knew he could always crash with his dad, but money would be a problem. At the time, he wasn't on speaking terms with his mother (for reasons too complicated to explain). Suddenly, his move to the tropics felt like a sink-or-swim proposition.

Although he didn't tell a soul, including Yair, David sort of agreed with his grandmother. Bula wasn't a particularly smart move.

"The whole enterprise was incredibly naive when you think about it," David said. "Both Yair and I left respectable careers to learn how to use a cash register and put boardshorts on plastic hangers." But David had already given Yair his solemn word that he'd fly to Aruba and check out the competition.

"I mean, how amazing was it that someone asked me to run a friendship-based shop in the Caribbean?" David recalled. "I really couldn't refuse."

David's father, aka Big Dave, also didn't initially warm to the idea of his son wasting his brains and talents on a surf shop. He struggled to make sense of the hopscotching: toss away a law school degree, gamble on a start-up in D.C., and hightail it to the Caribbean to shoulder the risks of starting a business.

Big Dave kept his apprehensions to himself . . . mostly. At one point, he urged David to reconsider. He hoped his son might figure out a way to parlay his law school training into a creative field compatible with his nontraditional upbringing. David listened to his father's concerns and reassured him he'd land on his feet, no matter what happened.

"I had to give him that," his father told me in a candid moment. "As a kid, he was scrappy as hell . . . had to be." Big Dave never forgot the day he had picked up David from the experimental boarding school his mother had found for him in North Carolina. He had shaved one side of his head. At the school, students were encouraged to learn by doing. They cut their own firewood. Dyed their hair weird colors. Did their own laundry, but not often. The dining hall was in a converted chicken house with a rusted metal roof. David slept on the second floor of a rickety cabin heated by a single wood stove. The water glass by his bed would freeze solid overnight. Fortunately, David had a mountaineering sleeping bag designed for subzero conditions.

"Okay, that whole school was pretty far out, as far as I was concerned," David's dad said. "But I knew if anyone could adapt, he could. He was a tough kid, and the divorce had made him tougher."

Reflecting back on David's decision to move to Aruba, his father can now connect at least some of the dots. "I'm sure he got permanently turned off by cold weather at that boarding school," Big Dave recalled. "He was a completely different kid that day he picked out his first skimboard in Wrightsville. I had a hard time getting him to leave."

When Yair told his parents he wanted to open a surf shop, they didn't at first believe him. They thought he was joking.

Yair's father had always hoped Yair might one day share his passion for business, but Yair expressed zero interest. What he didn't know about business, he didn't want to know. Yair had his own ideas of what a cool person did for a living—a vet, a geneticist, a jazz musician, perhaps. Definitely not a conservative business guy. As much as he respected his father's business acumen, Yair pegged himself as more of a creative type—not so unlike one of the Art 101 weirdos.

Yair's father, Adolf, was born in Aruba to poor Polish immigrants. As a kid, he rode a donkey to school. Adolf was brilliant, and his hardworking parents found the money to send him off to boarding school in the States and, later, Wharton Business School and NYU, where he earned a master's degree in finance. Adolf became a business pioneer in Aruba, opening up several retail and commercial enterprises. In the 1970s, he established Aruba's first department store, a two-story building with a small back office filled with the racket of secretaries punching in the cost of goods on manual typewriters.

Following in his father's giant footsteps just didn't feel legit to Yair. For years, he had fended off his father's gentle appeals to join him in the family business. He dreamed of marching to his own offbeat drummer. Then, early in 2002, sitting idly in the stargazing chair he had built, Yair had a startling vision. He was in the early stages of recovering from a bout with clinical depression.

"Every day I woke up and told myself I needed to regroup, go back to work, and become a productive member of society," he explained in one of our many one-on-one conversations. "I wasn't thinking about starting a business . . . the basics were beyond me. I didn't even know how to balance a checkbook."

Yair remembers glancing at his surfboard propped up against his parent's house. He'd just broken the board, and it bugged him that he had nowhere to go on the island to replace it. That was when he had his eureka moment. He imagined a shop filled with racks of gleaming surfboards and beautiful, functional items of clothing—all the gear surfers needed to enjoy the sport. He'd greet everyone as soon as they walked through the door, bookish or buff, young or old. Shop regulars would stay awhile, catching up on gossip, laughing, just hanging out.

Yair's fantasies of a mystical, perfect surf shop instantly lifted his spirits. A wave of relief washed over him, as if he'd woken up out of a troubling dream.

"Sure, I'd be running a retail business, but it wasn't as if I was managing a 7-Eleven or a Gap store," said Yair. "The surfing angle gave it a sexy, arty connotation." Yair continued, trying to paint a picture for me. "Like, a surf shop isn't the same as running a successful computer parts store." What lit him up was the chance to do something he truly believed in, while working side by side with his best friend. At the time, it all seemed so wonderfully simple.

As Yair mused to David, pre-Bula: "We spend most of our waking life at work. What better way to spend it than with people you love?"

"The Coolest Place on Earth"

Yair: We wanted to be authentic, whatever that really means. Being fake was a cardinal sin. It felt real to us to start a friendly surf shop for hardcore surfers.

David: There was a definite Gen-X flavor to Bula. We were obsessed with not selling out to someone else's idea of success.

Yair: Yeah, we're supposed to be a generation of slackers, right? Maybe we didn't have huge lofty goals like getting famous or making a fortune by a certain date. But we weren't at all afraid of the work.

David: We categorically didn't know what the hell we were getting ourselves into, but it's not as if learning retail is as difficult as building the Hadron particle collider. I had a chip in my head telling me a surf shop was the coolest place on Earth. Which proves what? I guess I wasn't so much motivated by high ideals or even basic self-interest but by middle-school fantasies.

Yair: Okay, let's run with that. I was just thinking about this. Both of us had, like, a very similar and possibly juvenile grasp on reality. We shared that ability to easily laugh at ourselves and pick up on absurd situations.

David: I mean, the whole Bula thing was a ridiculous thing to do with our potential. I left D.C. with such a loathing of being a lawyer. I'd rather wash dishes in a diner than work for a big law firm. There were so many other shit jobs I'd rather do. Some of my law school friends couldn't believe my stupidity. They were already making big salaries, killing themselves at work.

Yair: I remember dreaming about opening a place like an English pub where you walked in and people were happy to see you. They'd ask about school, your cousin, your mom. It really bothered me that no shops on the island paid much attention to the surfing community.

David: Yeah, we had all these idealistic dreams. We were about to spend practically every waking moment together, how naive was that?

Yair: Yeah, it never occurred to us that the whole thing might implode.

David: I suppose we inoculated ourselves against some of the classic pitfalls of friends in business just by talking stuff through early on. We understood we'd have to give each other some leeway in terms of money and budgets and learning curves. I also think, for some reason, I'm not sure why, culturally or genetically, we're not greedy people.

Yair: We definitely didn't have the get-rich-fast motive. If we could make enough money to cover our expenses and save a little, that would be enough. Up to that point, my parents had helped me out by paying for college and grad school. My father might have said, "I wish you had this realization before I put down all that college tuition." But he never said a word. I suppose he was just thrilled I finally wanted to do something halfway practical
. . . and better late than never.

Fishing with Ervin

When Yair was seven years old, he remembers fishing at Malmok Beach with the new Snoopy rod his father had just bought him. A young boy, Ervin Anaya, lived in a house facing the rocks where Yair was trying, in vain, to catch a monster fish. Noting Yair's struggles, Ervin walked right over, introduced himself, and offered his advice.

Malmok Beach is a popular snorkeling spot on the calm west side of the island. You often see boats at anchor a few hundred yards offshore, where divers explore the famous Antilla shipwreck.

"You're never going to catch anything with that huge hook," he told Yair. "There aren't any big fish here." Ervin tied on a small hook and handed the rod back to his new friend. Sure enough, Yair soon reeled in a grunt, a tiny fish all of five inches long. It was his first step toward the ultimate dream of catching deep-sea fish like yellowfin tuna, wahoo, and mahi-mahi.

"Ervin set me straight that day," said Yair. "We became best childhood buddies."

As a young adult, Ervin went to medical school in Bolivia. Whenever he returned to Aruba, he'd go surfing with Yair. Waiting in the lineup, they'd play their own private game of "Name That Disease." Yair quizzed Ervin on his medical cases and tried to guess the diagnosis. Back on shore, Ervin loved hearing Yair talk about "marine stuff, you know, intertidal ecosystems and wave patterns."

Yair celebrated when Ervin set up a pulmonology practice in Louisville, Kentucky, and Ervin was among the first Yair told about his plans for Bula Surf Shop. The news came as a bit of a shock.

"Aruba's a small society that's multicultural, but it can also get insular," Ervin told me. "I wasn't sure how Yair would deal with the intricacies of island politics."

Yair assured Ervin that he was going to be his own boss, set his own schedule, and basically either make it or not. He refused to let local politics hold him back. Ervin remembers the ring of conviction in Yair's voice. When Yair told him his girlfriend Ana had agreed to join him in Aruba, Ervin's reservations largely disappeared.

Yair's childhood dream of catching a trophy fish, like this yellowfin tuna, has come true many times over.

"Ana was his pillar," Ervin said. "She made it possible for him to stop searching [for a romantic partner] and concentrate on Bula."

Ervin now says he never truly doubted Yair would do well. "Bula was always about community, not prestige," he reflected. "Yair was interested in surfing and lifting up the whole culture of the island. He realized, long before I did, what would make him happy."

5

Risky Affairs of the Heart

Yair met Susanne (Ana) von Saalfeld in an elevator. They were both students in Miami, where she was finishing up her bachelor's in education. Yair remembers she propped open the door as he dragged the rest of his moving boxes into the small elevator. She'd just taught an infant swimming class, and her damp shorts and T-shirt reeked of the neighborhood pool. Just standing next to her, in their very own chlorine-scented pocket of elevator air, made his heart race. He stood very still, stiff as a piece of driftwood, and tried to think of something to say. Then Ana got off at her floor, and the doors shut behind her. *Don't go,* his mind said, *don't go.*

Neither of them thought they'd see each other again.

Luckily, a mutual friend spotted the matchmaking potential and invited them to hang out at his place. Ana led the conversation, regaling Yair with stories about growing up in Costa Rica and her love of swimming. As a teenager, she'd been a competitive swimmer at the national level. Yair listened spellbound when she talked about her latest dream of getting a degree and teaching on the international circuit.

Yair was "super shy," Ana told me. "There were these long, awkward silences. I thought he didn't like me." At the end of that first evening together, Yair pulled a creased photo out of his back pocket.

"That's the pier at Spanish Lagoon," he said, leaning toward her. "It's on the south coast of Aruba." Ana took a good look at the bright turquoise waters lapping the pier.

"Don't worry, one day you'll see it," Yair said with a confidence that surprised him. Ana moved closer and smiled with her whole body.

Ana and Yair visited her family in Costa Rica and toured La Paz Waterfall Gardens, a nature preserve with an amazing butterfly garden.

Yair and Ana gave me slightly different accounts of how they met, but there's no question the Spanish Lagoon photo set off the sparks of their early romance. After Yair left his gig in the Galápagos, he called Ana from Aruba to ask for a deeper commitment. He figured he had only the smallest chance of getting the answer he wanted, so he just blurted out the question.

"Hey, Ana. I want to open a surf shop in Aruba. Will you move down here to be with me?"

"Sure." Ana was sitting in her Miami apartment, fanning herself with a newspaper. She couldn't afford a rental with air conditioning.

"Yay, but really?" He worried she was teasing him.

"Sure, of course." She paused for a very long time. "But I'll need to find something to do."

"Okay," Yair said, relieved beyond measure. "I'll ask around at the international school."

"Cool," she replied. He could sense her happiness running toward him through the phone line.

"I'm a lucky guy," he said.

And that was that.

Like Yair, David had fond, if vague, memories of falling in love. He came up empty when I asked him about the time he asked his girlfriend, Debbie Kunder, if she'd move with him to Aruba.

"Hmm, better ask Debbie about all that," he told me. Fortunately, she shared the details of their romance with enthusiasm. For months they had hidden their secret crushes on each other from the circle of friends they partied with in D.C. As soon as they came out as an official couple, everything seamlessly fell into place. Debbie left a difficult roommate situation and moved her few possessions into David's apartment. Her stuff meshed with his. Even their unmated socks got along. Living in close quarters, she realized how deeply David despised working under the thumb of the government contractors who'd bought his company.

David and Debbie, early Bula days.

"He'd come home after work and sink down onto the sofa," she said. "Sometimes he'd start crying, and I tried to console him. But what could I do or say, really?"

Except for David's tortured job situation, those were happy times for them both. After growing up in a large, tight-knit Catholic family in Pennsylvania Dutch country, Debbie thrived on the urban scene and enjoyed her job at Georgetown University. Occasionally she took on modeling assignments to help with living expenses. At six feet tall, with her lean athletic build and wide-set blue eyes, Debbie looked like the fit young women you see scaling cliffs in active-wear catalogs. Eventually, she *was* one of those models.

Soon after she moved to D.C., Nike chose her for a catalog based on her ability to look flawless while dribbling a basketball. Later, a glossy magazine sent her on a shoot in a meadow where she hugged a horse in a field while modeling the latest in bridal fashion.

When David popped his question about moving to Aruba, he low-keyed it—no sinking down on bended knee or commitment speeches. The rosy haze of early infatuation had lifted by then, but they both knew it was way too early in the relationship for the "let's get married and settle down" discussion. Debbie didn't want or expect a marriage proposal. Plus, the idea of following her new boyfriend to the end of the world appealed to her romantic heart.

When Debbie and Ana said yes to Aruba, they each took a risky detour in their life path. Why on earth would two whip-smart, fun, and independent young women head to the southern Caribbean with hardly a question or backward glance? They'd have to pack up their comfortable routines and parachute into a strange new world, a place where giant iguanas skittered across the sidewalks and cacti grew as tall as two or three refrigerators stacked on top of each other.

Columnar cacti love Aruba's arid conditions. The thorns of this blue candle cactus form a neat row of rosettes. For scale: Xavi, a six-foot-tall Bula employee, peers up at the cluster of fans at the top.

Several species of lizards (lagdishi) thrive on the island. Ranging from neon green to sandy brown, iguanas roam freely on resort grounds, sun themselves on rocks, and make themselves at home in the trees. Photo credit: Dejavu Designs, dreamstime.com.

Debbie and Ana faced a heavy adjustment to life on a tiny desert island—just forty minutes by car from end to end—with no friends, family, or job prospects. And all those languages! Spanish was one thing, but what about Dutch? Then there was Papiamento, with its challenging mixture of Spanish, French, Portuguese, and Dutch, as well as Arawak and African influences.

I can only imagine how worried their parents must have felt seeing their daughters head out into the wild blue yonder with boyfriends they'd met only a short time before. David and Yair failed to meet the ideal of stable breadwinners. Yair was still in recovery from clinical depression, living with his parents. David, too, was in career limbo with no solid job prospects. And their big idea was starting a surf shop—with no discernible experience in retail. And then there were all the legal hassles: business licenses, visas, work permits. With money so tight, where would they live? And what if the relationships didn't survive all the pressures, then what?

None of it added up, objectively, to a brilliant plan.

"The Whole Idea of
Following Someone You Love . . .
I Think That's Beautiful."

Debbie (left) and Ana on a sunset stroll with their dogs.

Debbie and Ana didn't say no, not exactly, when I proposed a series of interviews about Bula. They acquiesced with one condition: Don't make this about us. Ana jokingly compared their backseat roles to the wives in the *Apollo 13* film who kept the home fires burning while their astronaut husbands performed heroics in space. Yet, both Ana and Debbie had plenty to say about their decision to follow the men they loved to the ends of the earth.

Ana: When Yair asked me to move to Aruba, he'd gone from the most grandiose save-the-ocean mentality to something completely different. He wanted to focus on something fun that probably wasn't going to work. Bula might last a couple years, and then it'd be over. That's the way most surf shops operated. The fact it worked out is kinda amazing.

Debbie: When I moved to Aruba, I never worried I'd lose out on a big career. Though I do remember a high school friend saying, "Well, I guess we just never expected our class valedictorian would end up sunning herself on some beach in Aruba." She had a point [laughing].

Ana: Yeah, well, I'm not a sit-on-the-beach sort of person either. I wanted to find work because I need consistency and purpose. Yair was wonderful about helping line up my first job, substitute teaching.

Debbie: I'm also definitely not the beach lover in my family. I remember thinking, *Living on a Caribbean island is wasted on me.* But when David said, "Come live with me," I said, "Yeah, sure!" The whole idea of following someone you love . . . I think that's beautiful.

Ana: When I was in Miami, missing Yair, I pictured him hanging out with the piles of driftwood in his parents' backyard. Unshaven, probably, and with unruly hair. Yair always lets his hair grow out until someone complains. He's definitely not a "comb my hair with gel" kind of guy. I like his casualness about his looks. We have this silly chemistry.

Debbie: It was the winter of 2003 when David and I moved to Aruba. We were used to seeing each other in sweaters, suits, and boots. It was the first time I'd ever seen him in surfing clothes. I thought he was so handsome, but I think that about him no matter what.

Debbie and David's view from their first rental apartment in Malmok, at sunset.

I remember holding hands with David as the sun set over the shipwreck in front of our first place. He kept his new windsurfing gear outside on a rack, so he could just grab it and head to the beach. It was a relief seeing him so happy.

Ana: When I first got to Aruba, I liked to pick up sea glass on the beach to make jewelry. I couldn't find the right epoxy. The earrings, they'd pop apart, very homemade. Yair made me a display stand to put by the cash register. I didn't know how to price anything. If someone showed enthusiasm, I got so excited. *Do you like these earrings? Here, take them!*

Debbie: I had a hard time adjusting at first. When my twin sister, Pattie, came to visit, we snorkeled and took the usual pictures of the sunsets and beaches. Anytime my family came to visit, we always had a really great time. Then I'd get depressed, and sometimes I cried after I dropped them off at the airport.

Ana: My friends didn't take my move to Aruba seriously. They thought of Aruba as Fantasy Island, some weird place where everyone's happy all the time. In the beginning, it was really hard to break in socially. Yair was working all the time, and Aruban families tended to hang out together in a tight bubble. Eventually I made some friends through Tai Chi and, later, at the international school where I got my first teaching job.

Debbie: Before I started homeschooling an American kid, I didn't know what to do with my time. At one point, I wanted to open a smoothie stand. Then I realized, it wasn't going to be cheap. Fresh fruit is expensive in Aruba . . . food in general is expensive. Everything gets shipped here on big cargo ships. And David and I didn't have any money. Our first rental was a little run down, but we really liked our landlady and her three kids. Sometimes we had trouble sleeping with the coconuts crashing down on the metal roof!

Ana: At first we lived in that apartment at Yair's parents' house. It was clear we'd have to find our own place. We liked the secluded Spanish Lagoon neighborhood, but rentals rarely came on the market. When we finally saw a house for rent, we were so excited we tore down the sign and threw it in the back of the car. Sentimentally, that place called out to us, we just *had* to have it!

Ana looks pensively out to sea in front of the first house
she and Yair rented, and later bought, in 2003.

The house was in disrepair, but it faced the same pier Yair showed me when we first met . . . amazing! We filled the rooms with his driftwood pieces—big chairs, tables, curvy toilet-paper holders. We had our very own Flintstone house [laughter].

Debbie: I remember how excited you were! That's when I was really getting into yoga. I had met a nice group of ladies from Holland, Britain, and some locals. I wasn't that close to you then.

Ana: Yeah, we weren't super close immediately. It was a different time. Since then, we've grown into a sisterhood.

In the 1996 romantic comedy *Jerry Maguire*, Tom Cruise echoed Plato's definition of true love when he announced to Renée Zellweger, "You . . . complete me." In that same spirit, David and Yair knew their dream of starting a surf shop wouldn't be complete without Debbie and Ana. From the start, Bula Surf Shop was a one-for-all, all-for-one proposition. Those weren't just empty words. Bula never would have gotten past the scribbles-on-a-napkin stage if Debbie or Ana had refused to join them in the adventure.

From a practical standpoint, David and Yair were supremely lucky that they found their life partners when they did. With Ana and Debbie by their side, they could channel their energy into building a business, not searching for a life partner. Still, the Aruba experiment changed both couples' choreography, introducing difficult new steps and routines.

David and Yair essentially said, "Let's step over here instead of there. Come with us, follow our lead. And even if we make mistakes, we'll figure it out. We've got this."

The simple truth: Ana and Debbie weren't about to shrink back or refuse the invitation to dance, even if the decision went against their immediate self-interest. They had fallen deeply in love. That one conviction overruled every other consideration. I imagine the decision was almost as automatic as a preprogrammed setting on a camera. Click, point, and shoot.

It seems weird looking at the situation from the outside because David and Yair didn't exactly have it all together, emotionally or professionally. Both of them were in a vulnerable place. They needed all the loving, emotional support they could get. Debbie and Ana gladly served the roles of two rescuers in a battle situation.

That's exactly what our friends are for, right? According to Joshua Greene, professor in the psychology department at Harvard University, the instinct to protect those we love goes back far into evolutionary history. Over thousands of years, people who favored their inner circle—whether a genetic relative or close friend—gained an advantage. Acts of cooperation allowed humans to outcompete rivals in times of danger or scarcity.

As Professor Greene says, friends have a "kind of reciprocity in a direct, face-to-face sort of way. . . . You'd share food with each other. You'd have each other's backs when going into battle, . . . take care of each other."[8]

As inexperienced business owners, David and Yair lacked the usual starter set of skills and tools; they didn't even have a nominal business plan. Bula was almost entirely fueled by the fumes of David's and Yair's youthful passion and idealism. If Ana and Debbie hadn't trusted them on a deep level, who knows what might have happened? It's impossible to imagine all the alternative scenarios. The crux of their decision, I suspect, stemmed from their faith in David and Yair. And that faith reminds me of my favorite definition of a close friendship: a friend is someone we can rely on, have fun with, and confide in.

David and Yair didn't suffer from the alienating, self-centered ambition of many youthful entrepreneurs. Bula sprang from collegial, homegrown roots. These friends simply wanted to run their own show, have fun, and do something cool to pay the bills. They scaled back expectations and didn't pretend to have every last detail locked down.

"Let's stay loose," they essentially said.

When Yair, David, Ana, and Debbie—Bula's pioneering tribe—took a flying leap into the bright blue yonder of the Caribbean, they set a fledgling dream in motion. Where it would take them was anyone's guess.

ACT II

6

Crazy Courage

On the way to Queen Beatrix International Airport, Yair mulled over his strategy for welcoming David to Aruba. He knew David would have tons of questions, and not just about the surf shop scene. Deciding whether to open a retail business was hard enough. An even dicier question was whether David could see himself living there, on a desert island roughly the size of Washington, D.C. Sure, David had spent time with his dad in the Bahamas and the Florida Keys, but they'd stayed at primitive fly-fishing lodges.

"I worried David might think Aruba was some uncivilized, Third World outpost," Yair told me.

David favored cosmopolitan places to live: the nation's capital, Miami, Tokyo. Like any tropical paradise, Aruba's provincial laid-back attitudes—charming at first—had a darker side. Need your roof repaired or your car fixed? Don't count on the carpenter or mechanic showing up on time. They don't stick to any schedule. Health care? Somewhat limited. Cost of living? High. You have to import almost everything and deal with customs. Then there's the culture shock of people smiling and saying hello, even strangers. Would the constant cheer get on David's nerves?

As soon as he spotted David outside at the arrivals exit, Yair tightened his grip on the steering wheel. David's face looked pale in Aruba's unfiltered sun. There wasn't a cloud in sight, just a vast dome of intense blue skies. The trade winds whipped the airport's stately palms into a frenzy of fronds.

Yair maneuvered his Mitsubishi truck into a pick-up spot and tapped the horn to get David's attention. David smiled, shouldered his duffle, and navigated through a sea of tourists. Yair crushed David in a bear hug and shoved aside an old beach towel to make room for the bag in the back of the truck.

As they drove toward downtown, Yair pointed out the sleek new grocery store. A couple of modern banks with ATMs stocked with crisp new American dollars. And a new French bistro that served onion soup with melted Dutch cheese and pastries on square plates.

That's where they made their first stop.

"This is a decent place to eat, right?" Yair said as they sat down at a marble-topped table by the window. A waitress brought them a carafe of water and two glasses. She welcomed them in English laced with a beguiling Dutch accent.

David sampled his chocolate croissant. "Really good," he said, taking a bigger bite.

Yair poured water into their glasses.

"I want to make a toast," he said, raising his glass high. "Welcome, my friend, to Aruba, home of the Balashi Cocktail." That's the locals' pet name for the water that gets desalinated, purified, and filtered at the state-of-the-art desalination plant in the Balashi region. In Aruba, drinking water flows from the tap—not plastic bottles—as pure as any in the world.

"Duly noted," David said, swiping his hand across his nose. Yair recognized the gesture. A swipe meant David was antsy.

"Want to get the show on the road?" Yair asked.

David nodded and pulled out his wallet. "My treat."

"Thanks, bro," Yair said as he pushed back his chair.

They motored north, windows wide open, along Aruba's main coastal roadway. On their left, the aquamarine sea gleamed. Spiny trees, twisted by the trade winds, grew out of the arid soil. A towering cruise ship, white and blue, glided by like a visiting skyscraper. It was another perfect day on the calm, leeward side of the island. Unlike other winter vacation spots, like Florida with its cold fronts, Aruba's weather is nearly always 85 degrees with a refreshing breeze.

Yair noticed David looking at the kites tangled in phone wires and stuck in trees.

"Yeah, we just had a kite-flying competition," Yair said. "If you live here for a while, the sight of a broken kite is pretty common."

The famous Fofoti trees on Eagle Beach have played starring roles in Aruba's advertising campaigns since the 1980s. Aruba's trade winds contort several species, including the inland Divi-Divi tree, permanently toward the west. Photo credit: Vilant, dreamstime.com.

In Aruba the wind picks up around Easter and stays strong until the end of June, conditions that explain the island's love affair with the kite. Most kites you see in Aruba, even the elaborate seven-footers, are fashioned from scarce resources and unfettered aspirations. In the Caribbean, kites have always served as a powerful source of self-expression.[9]

David closed his eyes and relaxed back into the passenger seat. The rhythmic beat of the Caribbean filled the car. The waves reliably rolled out to sea and back to shore with no human effort. A passing car blasted a catchy calypso tune from amped-up stereo speakers. Gauzy clouds, backlit by a fiery sun, traveled with them to their first stop: Beach Bum, Aruba's legendary old surf shop.

In the early 2000s, there was just a smattering of shops that stocked surfwear and equipment. Only one, Beach Bum, actually sold surfboards. Back then, Aruba's diehard surfers had to fly to the States to buy their boards, a real hassle. Choosing a surfboard is highly individual, a lot more complex than buying a pair of shoes. You need to match the board exactly to the rider's size, skill level, and preferred waves. At the popular surf breaks like you find at the Outer Banks of North Carolina or coastal California, shops stock a diverse selection of boards. Hundreds of them.

David ran his forefinger over the surface of the lone board on display at Beach Bum. "Could use a dusting," he whispered.

"This one's been here for a couple of years," Yair said, keeping his voice low. "He probably keeps it around as a prop." Beach Bum's middle-aged owner had never surfed a day in his life. His inventory of boards had gradually dwindled over the years. He'd probably lost hope that someone would buy the one he had left, though it wasn't much of a financial setback. Little-known fact: The profit from selling surfboards is razor thin. All the money is in beachwear—bikinis, sandals, boardshorts, and sunglasses.

"Pretty lame," David said, glancing around the store at the tired merchandise. Across the island, you'd see the same clothes on the rack, month after month. Beach Bum was no exception. Aruban shops generally lagged a couple of years behind the retail trends in the States. The shops could get away with a meager selection because of the limited competition. If a customer wanted an item the store didn't stock, it could take months to arrive. That's just the way it was. Local customers expected to wait.

Returning or exchanging an item wasn't a slam dunk either. Aruba hadn't caught up with the no-questions-asked exchange policies sweeping the States. Many shop owners still operated, proudly, from an antiquated model of service. If you bought a pair of sandals, most shops refused to give you a refund without a receipt, even the day after you bought them. Retailers rarely made exceptions to their store policies, even for wealthy tourists. Their inflexibility could come as a shock to shoppers from the States.

As a kid, Yair had seen shop owners treat locals differently. Lower-income Arubans often got indifferent service. Teenagers had it the worst, especially in the ritzy shops. Across the board, shops were set up to cater to tourists with a carefree holiday attitude about conspicuous consumption. Yair was passionate that Bula would fill a hole in the retail market—serving locals from all walks of life.

"Let's go," Yair said, cocking his head toward the door. They headed to the Royal Plaza Mall in Oranjestad, Aruba's capital city. A friend of Yair had given him a tip-off: The owner of Extreme Sports, a shop in the Royal Plaza Mall, was desperate to move to the Netherlands for undisclosed personal reasons. He wanted to liquidate his business. Although his retail space wasn't much bigger than a two-car garage, you couldn't beat the downtown location.

The Royal Plaza sits directly across the street from the cruise ship terminal in Aruba's prime downtown shopping district. Whether you stand on the deck of an incoming cruise ship or peer out an airplane window, you can glimpse the building's cotton-candy-pink walls and towering gold dome. The most spectacular view is by sea. As you glide into the dock at the cruise ship terminal, the Royal Plaza steals all the attention. With its ornate trellises, aqua awnings, and jolly pink exterior, the Royal Plaza isn't shy about flaunting its Dutch Caribbean roots.

A harbor view of the iconic Royal Plaza Mall,
the original home of Bula Surf Shop.

The Plaza has three levels with open-air walkways and sweeping views of the harbor. Extreme Sports occupied a nondescript storefront on the second floor. The owner enthusiastically showed them around the tiny space. Like newlyweds touring their first starter home, David and Yair had to look past the melamine slat paneling and interrogation-room overhead lights. In a matter of minutes, they had a handshake deal. Pending the usual legal entanglements, Bula would soon have a modest storefront to call its own, wedged between souvenir shops shouting the same lines: *Best 4 Less! Bikinis! Cigars!*

David and Yair weren't all that concerned about the optics. Finally, their dream was morphing into something tangible.

David had been in Aruba for less than forty-eight hours, and already he and Yair had their first lucky break—a retail space with a turnkey transfer of ownership for just $27,500 each. By most standards, it was a minuscule amount to pay for a start-up. Normally, it's difficult, expensive, and time-consuming to secure a retail license in Aruba. To celebrate, Yair took David to a nearby food truck. He recommended the oyster soup—rich, savory, and reasonably priced—with marinated onions and homemade *pica* (hot pepper sauce). As an added treat, they ordered the *pan calco*, a short stumpy single baguette loaded with stewed conch.

"Good you have an iron stomach," Yair said, as his truck lurched over the rocks and ruts on the way to Wariruri Cove.

Yair had promised David he'd take him to his favorite surf break on the windswept north coast. For two rookie retailers with dreams of opening an authentic surf shop, the beach was a symbolically perfect destination. At Wariruri, there are no amenities within miles. You need a 4x4 vehicle to get there. Once you arrive, you're rewarded by strong currents, a small cobblestone beach, and a sign warning swimmers and snorkelers about the hazards.

"For locals, surfing at the north shore is a point of pride," Yair said. "If it's even remotely surfable, you go out, no matter what."

Most non-Aruban surfers would deem the conditions, most days, unfit for surfing. The unobstructed trade winds on the windward eastern side of the island produce messy, choppy waves. Rather than breaking smoothly, with a glassy face, Aruba's waves are disorganized and hard to read, even for experienced surfers. For all these reasons, surfers in Aruba watch out for each other. They're an unusually tight-knit micro community.

As the truck hit another rut, David remembered saying to Yair, "We can outcompete the other shops because we actually surf." He finished his thought in a rush of words. "We're young. We're interested in surfing. We're connected to what's cool."

No brass band or thunderbolt marked the occasion. The ancient volcanic ledge under their feet didn't shift. But Yair sensed, at that precise moment,

David felt the same heat he did—a vision only they could see. Bula was more an attitude than a decision they could rationalize. Passion and youthful courage pushed them forward, propelled by an underlying certainty: They couldn't *not* do this thing.

"Making the Drop"

David: Everyone was, like, super excited when we told them we wanted to open up a real surf shop, with real equipment. Because they didn't like having to go to Miami for a board.

Yair: That friendliness, it's not typical, right? At the popular surf breaks—you know, places like Hawaii, California, and the Gold Coast of Australia—you're lucky if the locals don't throw rocks at your windshield or slash your tires. If you're a kook or drop in on someone, things can get nasty. There's just so much competition in the lineup for a good wave. In Aruba, surfers are more of a family. The conditions are so messy and unpredictable. You get automatic respect for just paddling out.

David: When we showed up at the beach, it was just so friendly. I remember the banter and the backslapping.

Yair: Well, I grew up with a lot of those guys.

David: I don't want to underestimate the welcoming-ness, if that's a real word.

Yair: Yeah, but that's the culture here.

David: A couple of surfers came right over and asked where I was from. I got the halo effect of being your friend.

Yair: I definitely remember thinking you might actually like living here.

David: Aruba was pretty much love at first sight . . . a better path for me. I was staring down the barrel of having to get a white-collar job in D.C. Opening a surf shop seemed fun and exciting by comparison. In retrospect, Bula probably wasn't the *greatest* idea. But there was a moment when I thought, *Okay, why not? Let's do this.*

Yair: Our timing was lucky, right? We had the benefit of being relatively young guys who loved to surf at a time when surfing was at its peak of hipness. The mega brands like Quiksilver were killing it in the early 2000s. Even people who didn't own a board or even live near the ocean wanted to look like a surfer. There was that mystique of the wave rider. Surf brands were shipping mass quantities of merchandise to the mall stores while pretending they weren't part of a billion-dollar industry.

David: Yeah, we didn't want to open a surf shop in name only. You know, just to sell stuff.

Yair: The community angle seemed so clear at the time. If you were a retailer and saw a hungover surfer type or skateboarder come into the shop, you ignored them. We wanted to shake things up . . . like, give the rowdies a welcoming vibe.

David: All the business risks were there, but we didn't see them, starting with how we'd make enough sales to keep the doors open.

Yair: We didn't know how ignorant and naive we really were.

David: We were like the idiots who assume surfing is super easy. They think: *You just go out, get up on the board, shred a little, and then you have a barbecue at the beach later.* We had the same degree of cluelessness about retail. The surf metaphor might be "making the drop," right? When you decide to go for a wave, the harder you paddle, the better off you're going to be. Holding back or timidity can be a recipe for disaster, leaving you hung up in the lip, with the inevitable slam to follow.

Yair: Good one, Dave.

You may remember, I remarked on Bula's resemblance to a Purple Cow in the Introduction. It's a rich topic, worth a deeper look. In late 2002, Penguin Books published a slender book called *Purple Cow: Transform Your Business by Being Remarkable.* The author, an outspoken pundit named Seth Godin, urged companies to stop playing it safe. Winners separate themselves from the herd, he wrote. They're the purple cows in a field of monochrome Jerseys. Godin defined a Purple Cow as anything counterintuitive, surprising, exciting . . . remarkable. Every day, consumers overlook the brown cows, he said, but you can bet they won't ignore a Purple Cow.

Godin's slim book hit the bestseller lists in 2003 and became a must-read for entrepreneurs and marketers. I bought the original edition, with its distinctive purple cover. When the updated version came out in 2009, with a bonus section, I bought that too. Godin forever changed my views about the traditional Ps—positioning, product, pricing, promotion, and publicity. As a brand strategist, I'd always considered them sacrosanct until Godin made his case for the most important P of all: Purple Cow.

When I first heard David and Yair talk about their early plans for a friendly little surf shop, I visualized a field of brown cows—the other touristy beach shops at the time—and Bula, a future Purple Cow. What was so remarkable about their concept? Paradoxically, Bula was a throwback.

The original surf shops, dating back to the late 1950s, sprang up in nondescript garage spaces where a hot local surfer both shaped the boards in the backroom and worked the counter. Locals filed in to shoot the breeze, check out the latest merchandise, and soak up the vibes of coolness. In these early days, a surf shop served a dual function as a cultural watering hole and a place to buy gear.

This was the ethos David and Yair wanted for Bula. No other retailer on the island had that vision because they weren't surfers. They didn't care about surfing. As surfers themselves, David and Yair had a good sense of what locals wanted and needed. Boardshorts that were both stylish and functional. A decent selection of boards suitable for local surfing conditions. A good selection of surf wax. They had a hunch Bula could compete on product coolness.

But exciting products alone don't make a Purple Cow. You have to be *inherently* purple, according to Godin. Otherwise, people will lose interest in your shiny new toys. They won't care enough to come back or spread the word. Bula's "purpleness" stemmed from deep cultural roots rather than physical products.

Thinking as fired-up young entrepreneurs, David and Yair spotted an opportunity to increase the happiness of a marginalized group of consumers: surfers, skateboarders, and other lovers of ocean sports. Although other retailers didn't actively discriminate against these customers, they saved their lavish attention for the wealthier patrons.

"Entrepreneurship appears to be almost wholly dependent on a sense that the present order is an unreliable and cowardly indication of the possible. The absence of certain practices and products is deemed by entrepreneurs to be neither right nor inevitable, but merely evidence of the conformity and lack of imagination of the herd." [10]

ALAIN DE BOTTON, BRITISH AUTHOR AND PHILOSOPHER

To be clear: Giving preferential treatment to certain people and not others isn't unique to Aruba nor any society. Harvard professor Mahzarin Banaji has spent years studying implicit bias, the blind spots wired into human behavior. Favoritism, a subtle form of bias, often flies under the radar. We may have gotten a job interview because the hiring manager went to the same school or done a favor for someone because we had friends in common.

According to Professor Banaji, we often interpret these acts of prejudicial treatment as examples of generosity or kindness. Rarely do we consider the costs of favoritism. For every person at the receiving end of favoritism, there is another who's excluded from the same advantages. Consider the patients who wait longer in the emergency room or get basic treatment while a celebrity patient receives VIP medical care. There's a societal cost to favoritism.

As idealists, Yair and David asked themselves a crucial question: What if we treated everyone the same? Earlier, they had posed another deceptively simple question: What if we put friendship first? Those two principles together help explain why Bula Surf Shop had a fighting chance at achieving Purple Cow status.

David and Yair weren't interested in competing head-to-head with other retailers. That's the point of the Purple Cow. You stake out your own competitive territory. In Bula's case, they went for an underserved group of consumers at the fringes of the retail scene and built a business faithful to their friendly lifestyle ideals.

7

The Stink of Newbies

David remembers the excitement of packing for the January 2003 Surf Expo in Orlando, the largest in the world. Later that month, he would pack up his possessions, what little he had, and take a one-way flight to his new home base in Aruba. He felt like an explorer on the brink of discovering a new world—exhilarated and intensely focused.

For the telecom conventions he used to attend, David had packed with a heavy heart: his best blazer, silk tie, and lace-up Oxford shoes. Most of the attendees were paunchy, middle-aged executives in pinstriped suits. David looked forward to the ultra-athletic vibe at Surf Expo. Surfer style emphasizes minimalism—lightweight, drip-dry clothing and slip-on footwear. For his foray into the surfing industry, David figured he could get away with an upscale version of the rubber flip-flop. He wore his leather Reef sandals, the same pair he wore the day he met Yair in art class.

David had coordinated his travel plans with Yair, who would fly from Aruba and meet him at Orlando's cavernous convention center.

"We went to Surf Expo thinking we would be, like, treated as heroes by the industry because we loved surfing and had plans to set up a real surf shop," David told me. "We thought everyone would say, 'Wow, that's awesome!'"

Back in 2003, Surf Expo was a sprawling, three-day extravaganza with movie screenings, ear-piercing live music, and acres of exhibitor booths. More than 850 companies congregated at the cavernous convention hall to showcase their latest innovations. Besides surfboards and apparel, exhibitors promoted wetsuits, harnesses, car racks, cameras, watches, and video games.

At private parties, attendees consumed prodigious quantities of alcohol. Some exhibitors spent most of the three days either inebriated or hung over.[11]

Surf Expo had its wild side, but for industry veterans, it meant serious business. Millions of dollars changed hands. Top buyers checked out the new lines, cozied up to the brand reps, and ordered the next season's merchandise. The major brands could afford to be discriminating, only selling to shops with a compatible brand image and deep pockets.

David and Yair didn't have a formal game plan for their first Expo other than wild-eyed immersion. Wearing their plastic ID tags, they wandered up and down the exhibitor aisles. Long-limbed models with incandescent smiles and perfect tans glided by in tiny bikinis. At the big exhibitors—Billabong, Quiksilver, and Volcom—they witnessed a frenzy of buying and selling. As greenhorn retailers, they got the brush-off from almost everyone.

"We really didn't know what to ask or say," remembered Yair.

"Yeah, we had the stink of newbies," David agreed.

They occasionally caught the attention of a junior booth worker who listened long enough to realize they had little money to spend. No A-listers wanted to waste their time answering the questions of a couple of rank amateurs with vague plans.

"We got a lot of swag that way," Yair said. "The rep would lose interest and get rid of us by handing us a key ring or bottle opener. It was our cue to get lost."

They got their ultimate brush-off at the Quiksilver exhibit. Founded in 1973 in Australia by two surfers, Quiksilver was the industry's most successful maker of surfwear, wetsuits, and surfing accessories. In early 2003, international sales totaled more than $1 billion, a first for the surf industry. Like the other major exhibitors, Quiksilver created an inner sanctum for serious buyers. Models strutted back and forth on a runway, retailers leafed through catalogs, and reps wrote orders for the upcoming season.

David and Yair remember battling a crowd to get in front of the Quiksilver gatekeeper on duty. With his laminated name badge and powerful build, the vibes were none too cordial.

"Do you have an appointment?" he asked, glancing at his clipboard.

"No, we just want to talk to someone," Yair said, smiling.

"Yeah, we're opening a surf shop in Aruba," added David.

The mention of the Caribbean, a relatively small retail market, didn't win them any points.

"We don't have a Caribbean rep here," he said, glancing behind them at the people waiting in line. "Sorry."

Under the glare of the fluorescent lights, David and Yair wandered the aisles. The scent of hot dogs turning on greasy rollers lured them to a food vendor in a corner of the convention hall. They sat down on folding chairs, ate chili dogs, and watched a skateboard exhibition. During a break in the action, they collected their bags of swag and set out for the booth of a mid-tier surfwear brand called Rusty.

Although Rusty didn't have the cachet of the major brands, David and Yair admired its authentic pedigree. Rusty Preisendorfer, a legendary surfboard shaper, had founded the company in 1985 based on his ideals of risk taking and personal freedom. When the rep greeted them with a smile, they almost couldn't believe it. They'd come braced for another put-down. The Rusty booth wasn't exactly a beehive of activity, but still. The booth worker took his time with them, answering their questions, and got them set up with an account.

"He was the only one who didn't immediately size us up as complete yahoos," David told me.

"Yeah, shout out to Rusty," added Yair.

The Surf Expo wasn't a complete wipeout. After their uplifting experience with the Rusty rep, they established accounts with a skateboard distributor and Spy sunglasses. Every awkward relationship they forged at Surf Expo would come in handy when it was time to stock Bula's empty shelves.

I asked David and Yair if their first Surf Expo left any lasting psychological scars or blunted their passion for starting a surf business. Did they leave early and dump their bags of swag in the trash? Or worry and lose sleep?

"It didn't take long to realize we weren't as cool as we thought," said Yair. "We were inordinately grateful when anyone paid attention to us."

David and Yair's memories of the Expo reminded me of how athletes talk about practice and how actors approach rehearsal. Pre-Bula was a period of intense focus, trial and error, and rapid learning for two retailers with no industry experience. David and Yair shrugged off the put-downs of Surf Expo as the necessary precursor to opening a shop. Like beginners in a game of tennis, both players expected to hit some lame shots. Still, their egos and confidence took a hit.

In *How I Built This: The Unexpected Paths to Success from the World's Most Inspiring Entrepreneurs*, Guy Raz argues that starting a business "can be lonely, full of ups and downs that are hard to stomach when you're on the entrepreneurial roller coaster by yourself."[12] His advice: Make sure you have someone to brainstorm with and cheer you up when things go off the rails. The low points in a start-up are so low, Raz writes, few can bear them alone. Luckily, Bula's founders were never alone.

David and Yair still commiserate about the buffeting they took at their first Surf Expo. Two decades after opening the shop, they now get daily requests from start-ups that want Bula to carry their merchandise.

"We always try to be cordial," Yair said. "We remember the humiliation of getting shunned by the big guys."

Nothing Worse than a Sellout

As Generation Xers, born in the mid-seventies, David and Yair are members of a relatively small demographic cohort known as the Slacker Generation. Gen Xers conjure up images of angst-ridden dropouts with long, unwashed hair and lackluster ambitions. Authenticity, being true to self, motivates them, as not much else does. If Gen Xers excel at anything, it's apathy. When accused of lacking gumption, the stereotypical response is a shrug. Or nothing at all.

Of course, it makes no sense to pin a single label on sixty-six million people. But we are all shaped by the waters we swim in; sometimes the broad stereotypes do apply. Growing up in the nineties, David and Yair developed a distaste for people willing to don suits and sell their souls to a corporation. As Chuck Klosterman quipped in his bestselling book, *The Nineties*: "The mid-nineties were a time when an authentic jerk was preferable to a likable sellout."[13] In the spirit of the times, both David and Yair took a sharp turn away from conventional careers that made them feel like well-paid sellouts.

Their contemporaries climbing the corporate ladder were stunned: Why would two educated guys trade in good careers for a sketchy life as surf bums? In popular use, the term "surf bum" implies a lack of discipline, real or perceived. If a nonsurfer calls someone a surf bum, it's a surefire term of contempt. But when hardcore surfers talk about a surf bum, they intend it as praise.

"I'm a surf bum," Kahuna says in the 1959 movie *Gidget*. "You know, ride the waves, eat, sleep, not a care in the world." As Matt Warshaw writes in *The Encyclopedia of Surfing*, when surfers describe themselves as surf bums, they use the phrase with affection or irony.

As aspiring entrepreneurs, David and Yair endured many bummer days, brush-offs, and put-downs. But I seriously doubt anyone who knew David and Yair well ever worried they'd spiral down the food chain and live out their days as surf bums, surrounded by empty beer cans and pizza boxes.

8

Rookie Mistakes

"We need a spreadsheet," David said, looking at Yair. They were in full prep mode for opening day.

David reminisced with me about how he'd squatted on the floor of Bula's empty retail space, sipping coffee he'd bought from the friendly lady downstairs who owned the coffee kiosk.

"What?" Yair asked. He was busy with a broom, stirring up a dust storm.

"All our numbers will be wild estimates for our entertainment only," David explained. "You know, a precision planning document based on half-assed guesses of what we'll need to pay for inventory and getting the shop ready."

They'd randomly set April 7, 2003, for Bula's opening day. As two well-educated guys, they figured they'd have plenty of time. Mind you, their only retail experience was shopping at other people's stores. They knew nothing about pricing, ordering, displays, or promotion.

"Yeah, sounds good." Yair went back to sweeping the floor. The previous owner had left behind a trail of store receipts, a scuffed-up *I Love Aruba* keychain, and a bent pair of cheap kid's sunglasses.

"We'll need a Bula sign out front," David said.

"And new light fixtures and door hinges, stuff like that," Yair added. "I can make hanging racks." He leaned on the broom and looked around, imagining the racks suspended from the ceiling.

"Driftwood?" David asked.

"'Course."

Yair loved visualizing how the surfing apparel would look on the racks. He envisioned a chill, do-it-yourself vibe: a set of racks suspended on ropes and held together with plumbing pipes and bolts. Filling the racks with clothes was the bigger hurdle. Normally, retailers order months ahead from the big brands. After their poor showing at the Orlando Surf Expo, David and Yair had made an appointment with Paul, the owner of a beachwear boutique in Coconut Grove, Florida.

"I like you," Paul assured them. "I'll give you a deal on merchandise." Like a realtor pointing out the upgrades in a model home, he took them on a tour of the bikinis, shirts, and boardshorts. His hyped-up enthusiasm proved contagious. David and Yair purchased a mash-up of clothes in different sizes and from mixed brands. One polka-dot bikini of one brand, a large red and two mediums in a competitor's line.

"We thought it was the score of the century," Yair told me. Paul had sold them enough clothes to fill three large duffel bags.

"Really, we were just a couple of gullible assholes," David added. "Selling us apparel at cost plus 10 percent was Paul's way of getting rid of all the stuff that wasn't selling."

Technically, the transaction qualified as a breach of contract. Paul acted as a reseller, and that's forbidden in the retail business. When you sign a contract with a major brand like Billabong, you aren't supposed to resell the merchandise. David and Yair were clueless about the ethical violation and left Paul's shop in excellent spirits.

As they walked out of the refrigerated chill into the Florida heat, David and Yair congratulated each other on a productive outing. Their overstuffed duffels felt good and weighty on their shoulders as they headed to the Miami airport. Already Bula's future looked a little brighter.

To meet their tight timeline for opening day, they ordered an initial batch of T-shirts from a Colombian supplier recommended by a friend of Yair. Carlos was a sweaty, nervous guy with an ashen pallor. He took his time answering all their questions and even offered them a price break if they added stickers to the order. After they nailed down the details, he asked for full payment, up front. With no other options and time running out, David and Yair wrote a check for $3,000. At the time, it was a king's ransom.

As soon as the money cleared, Carlos made a string of lame excuses about why he couldn't return their calls. Back then, with spotty internet and landline phones, ghosting was much easier. He'd pull a disappearing act for days at a stretch. David and Yair started to worry, but Carlos was always so friendly when he got back in touch.

Then one day a cousin of Carlos stopped by the store. He acted shocked that David and Yair hadn't heard the news. Carlos was in rehab in Colombia. Too late, David and Yair put all the troubling clues together.

Their order had vanished into the ether.

David told me he'd felt vaguely seasick as he glumly entered the $3,000 loss into his spreadsheet.

"What a dick," he muttered.

"Yeah," Yair said. "Now we know we shouldn't give cash to an addict so he can blow it on cocaine in Colombia."

"It's just like when you put your hand on a hot stove," David said. "Unless you're a total idiot, you don't do that again."

They talked faster and faster as they brainstormed ideas for recouping their financial loss. They felt better after tinkering with the estimates in their spreadsheet. Rather than pay someone to put up the wallpaper, for example, they'd decided to do it themselves. How hard could it be?

For the April opening, Yair and David decided that Bula would need at least a dozen surfboards to pass muster as a true surf shop. Surfers accumulate boards for different conditions, not unlike a collection of fishing rods. Surfers in Aruba typically ride high-performance shortboards, since they work better in Aruba's choppy waves. They're called shortboards to distinguish them from the longboards that run eight feet or longer. A longer board is ideal for surfing the long, gentle waves you find in Costa Rica or Malibu.

Once you're on a wave, a smaller board gives you more maneuverability. You can more easily change direction. The drawback of smaller boards is their lack of flotation. If you're starting out in surfing, just getting on a wave is extremely difficult. The smaller the board, the more it sinks, making it harder to catch the wave. The longer boards have more flotation, so they are easier to paddle and glide more easily.

"Starting out, you definitely want a bigger board," Yair explained to me. "With the extra width and volume, you learn faster and get less frustrated."

Invariably, beginning surfers buy boards too small for them. "Kids often want to buy the same equipment they see their favorite pros riding in the surf videos," added David. "It's hard to talk them out of it."

If you buy too small a board, it's a lot more difficult to generate speed. When you stand up on a board, pushed by a wave, you need to start "moving down the line" away from the part of the wave that's crumbling. A bigger board with more flotation makes that easier. The board naturally planes and travels forward, while a smaller board will want to sink. If you're skilled, you use the energy of the wave to position the board so that it naturally picks up speed. If you're unskilled, you sink fast. To compensate, rookie surfers on too-small boards often develop bad habits. They hop and move their arms spastically, flailing about. It makes for a very unnatural style.

That's the big thing in surfing—the style.

"You want to look smooth and efficient," Yair warned me. "Not like you're having an epileptic seizure on the board."

Yair knew someone in Brazil who could get Bula surfboards in time for opening day. Ordering custom boards typically takes months, so David and Yair had decided on an assortment of readily available boards that they would be able to sell for just under $400 each. That's a bargain-basement price point, in the gutter really. David and Yair expected the locals wouldn't want to spring for more expensive boards. It was a serious miscalculation.

Ditto, about skateboards.

Another buddy of Yair, an excellent skater, told them they'd need to stock up on skateboards. He, too, didn't think Bula would sell many surfboards, and no shops in Aruba sold skateboards. It was an easy decision to go heavy on the skateboard selection.

Yair's skater friend, a self-professed expert, gave them explicit instructions: Order this, not that.

David and Yair mulled it over and decided they'd split the inventory evenly: 50 percent surfboards, 50 percent skateboards. On the surface, they made a sensible decision. Bula was close to the local skate park, so that augured well for attracting a crowd. The locals they knew—Bula's de facto test market—gave them a thumbs-up on the skateboards. But everyone had conflicting opinions on what brands and styles to buy.

As with surfboards, skateboards come in a complex variety of shapes, sizes, and price points. The best skateboards for everyday street skating have nearly symmetrical popsicle-shaped decks or boards. Street skaters typically prefer smaller narrow decks (8.0–8.5 inches) because they make it easier to do tricks. Pro riders can tell, just by touch, if a board is out of alignment by even a fraction of an inch. Beyond the function and feel of a well-balanced board, the graphics make the sale. Yair and David had no way of knowing which deck designs would appeal to Aruban teenagers. So they pored over the catalogs and made selections based on their gut reactions.

They eliminated decks featuring sexualized Japanese anime schoolgirls in lurid colors.

"We had our minimal standards," David assured me. Murder scenes, dragons eating elephants, and other explicit or violent scenes got ruled out, too. They selected tasteful arty designs, figuring those would fit Bula's laid-back aesthetic and bring buyers through the door.

They figured wrong.

"We Didn't Know What We Didn't Know"

David: Do you remember why we chose April 7 to open?

Yair: Nope, no clue. Maybe because it was a Monday.

David: We'd always make snap decisions and congratulate ourselves on our decisiveness.

Yair: If we couldn't figure something out, we'd take the advice of self-proclaimed experts.

David: Right. That's why, weirdly, skateboards were the most professionally stocked category when we opened. We probably had forty decks displayed, along with a decent selection of trucks, wheels, bearings, etc. But it's bizarre because the skater we trusted knew nothing about running a skate shop. The advice we got from him we should have ignored. We didn't know any better.

Yair: Yeah, we didn't know what we didn't know. We improvised as best we could, but really sucked at it.

David: Starting out in retail seemed pretty simple: Figure out what you need to sell every day, or else you'll lose money and go out of business.

Yair: But even the basics eluded us. The reps kept hammering into our thick skulls: fold your T-shirts and shorts and put them out on a shelf or table so people could see the designs. But I was stubborn . . . I wanted to put all the clothes sideways on hangers, like records lined up in a music store.

David: I suppose we thought we were just a little too smart for retail. We figured our education and intelligence were a fine substitute for a lack of experience. So we made decisions that weren't based on much except random hunches and logic that made no sense to anyone else.

Yair: Most people spend at least three years working in other people's stores before opening their own. They learn the basics of running a retail business. Then they open a store. We skipped the driver's ed class and just hit the road at ninety miles an hour.

9

Life's Swell

Imagine taking a new job where you're expected to thrive in a fast-paced environment and deal diplomatically with customers. Pretty standard, right? But now let's say the position also requires you to acclimate to Caribbean beach culture and love the sport of surfing. Might you have creeping doubts it wasn't a real paying gig?

When David moved to Aruba in early 2003, he sometimes wondered if he'd walked onto a movie set. He went from fighting D.C. Beltway traffic to an easy commute on a serene coastal road edged by seas so vibrant they looked photoshopped. His winter work clothes got replaced by drip-dry boardshorts and a rotation of lightweight T-shirts. Every morning, he'd brew a fresh pot of coffee and get dressed for the day in a state of near euphoria. Even his trusty navy-blue Volvo seemed happier in Aruba. Instead of carrying his leather briefcase and an ice scraper, his soccer-mom wagon transported a surfboard and a water jug for washing the sand off his feet before heading to work.

Soon after David moved to Aruba, Yair again took him to Wariruri Cove. The trip wasn't a casual outing. They both knew David would need to become proficient as a wave rider if Bula stood a chance at establishing its authenticity as a true surf shop.

The learning curve in surfing is incredibly steep, and it's best to start young. Although David didn't learn to surf as a kid, he had one advantage. Growing up, he'd spent a lot of time on and around the water.

"Maybe it was genetic, coming from my dad," he said. "From the time I was old enough to walk, we'd go out on boats, fishing and diving, and in every imaginable weather condition." When David went to law school in D.C., he used to windsurf in the polluted Potomac because he missed being on the water. A lifetime accumulation of these experiences gave him a leg up. He understood waves break in different directions and have unique personalities. The ability to read wave patterns is a cardinal skill of any surfer.

Aruba's waves present a higher-than-average challenge for a novice like David. Constant trade winds make it blustery. Wind-generated waves come close together. They're choppier, less well-organized than the long, smooth gliders you see at breaks at Malibu or Waikiki.

"Learning to surf in Aruba is about the hardest type of learning," Yair told me. "Maybe that's why, as a kid, I gravitated toward windsurfing and diving." But once Ervin, his childhood friend, challenged him to take up surfing, Yair got hooked. Nothing stopped him, not even his frequent trips to the emergency room—broken teeth, gashes requiring stitches, meniscus tears. One day Yair took a fin to the face. He rushed to the hospital with flaps of skin hanging down over his nose and lacerations to his eye socket.

"Pretty much everyone who surfs gets banged up," he added. "There's no way to avoid it."

On David's first outing, Yair gave his friend a few pointers from the safety of the shore. Two or three other surfers were there that day, all friends of Yair. As hardcore surfers, they made the basics look easy, but paddling out into the sea takes skill, power, and endurance. Experienced paddlers are amazingly fast and can cover extensive areas, improving the odds of catching a good wave.

Even waiting for a wave in the lineup of other surfers requires finesse and know-how. You don't want to paddle directly into the heart of the lineup. If you take a straight shot, you'll risk paddling in front of a surfer in position to catch a wave. Interfering with another surfer's priority is a big violation in surfing. Surfers often survey the lineup from the beach and figure out their best approach before paddling out.

That day at Wariruri, Yair walked David through a core surfing technique: the duck dive. Duck diving requires that you push the nose of the surfboard under an incoming wave with your arms while dipping below the passing wave—a difficult maneuver for beginners. Skilled wave riders build up speed and glide under the wave with dolphin grace. Less experienced surfers often hesitate, understandably, when they see a gigantic wave coming at them.

If you freeze and stop paddling, the energy of the wave will suck you under and bob you around. It's like pedaling a bicycle too slowly. You wobble and fall over. A similar problem can strike when surfers sit on the board while getting pushed around by the waves. If they don't pay attention, they become unbalanced and topple over.

Style matters a great deal in surfing circles, so Yair warned David about another standard kook maneuver. When they're just starting out, novices balance themselves too far back on the board. Other surfers can identify them as beginners when they paddle with the nose of the board pointed too high out of the water.

David remembers thinking he'd catch on faster than he did. He was a strong, confident swimmer and had no fear of being out in rough conditions. He wasn't afraid of looking uncoordinated or even getting pulled under after one of his frequent wipeouts. But in the first few weeks, just paddling the board exhausted him. The overstressed muscles in his back, shoulders, and arms would turn leaden and unresponsive. The condition is so common that surfers coined a term for it—*spaghetti arms,* also known as "rubber arms" or "noodle arms."

Like all beginners, David also struggled to keep his balance on the board, waiting in the lineup. The humiliations seemed endless, but he quickly picked up on one of the golden rules of surfing etiquette: If you accidentally get in someone's way, apologize. Even if you're unsure who's at fault, apologize. At least it shows that you know you're aware of your shortcomings and trying hard.

Surfers may strike you as a mellow bunch on land, but on the water, life can get dicey fast, even in laid-back Aruba. Fortunately, the codes of conduct make intuitive sense: Don't snake (paddle in front of a surfer to get closer to the peak), drop in (steal someone's wave), or ditch your board when a monster wave comes out of nowhere.

One of David's go-to surfboards. A couple years after he moved to Aruba, David got stabbed in the side by a board, necessitating an emergency trip to the hospital and multiple stitches.

Most surfboards are hard objects with sharp fins. Surfers who abandon their boards out of fear or inexperience can do serious harm to other surfboards or nearby people. As a beginner, it's best to put yourself outside the strike zone of other surfers. A buffer will lessen the risks if you lose control of your board—and your cool.

A week or so into his surfing career, David was about to paddle out when he felt a pinprick on his left foot, a mild shock. When he turned around and walked back to shore, Yair knew something was wrong. "I guess I stepped on something nasty," he recalls telling Yair.

They both peered at his middle toe. Neither could see a mark, but soon the pain radiated like an electric fire from David's left foot up the side of his body and all the way to his face.

"Okay, let's go," Yair said. He helped David get to the truck and drove like a maniac, lights flashing, to the hospital. As they raced to the ER, David's skin got warm to the touch, and his left foot swelled alarmingly. All the symptoms pointed to a severe allergic reaction to a scorpion fish. As menacing as they look, with their large spiny heads and dorsal spikes, scorpion fish don't attack unless provoked. Their toxic venom rarely causes life-threatening symptoms, but the pain can be excruciating.

David told me he can't remember much of what happened at the ER. As the fiery pain worsened, he lost all sense of time and place. The only thing he definitely remembers is Yair pacing in the waiting room and checking in repeatedly with the staff.

David had never been in a hospital before, not even for his tonsils or a broken bone. His mother didn't believe in traditional medicine, so he'd never seen a doctor either. When he went to his first traditional school, the George School in Pennsylvania, he needed to present a health certificate. His mother arranged for a chiropractor to sign the medical form.

"They probably gave her a religious exemption or something," David explained when I expressed surprise.

"David's dream society was Japan, with its strict rules and smooth-running public services," Yair added. "I worried the inefficiencies of the ER experience would make him question his decision to move here."

David told me he has no recollection of the hospital's handling of his scorpion fish sting but does remember Yair's rising annoyance.

"I just thought he was being his usual overprotective self," David said. "I didn't realize he had all these existential concerns that I'd freak out about not getting seen right away."

When David hobbled out of the ER, Yair stayed glued to his side. A friendly Dutch doctor had given David a shot and antibiotics. He immediately felt a lot better. His first visit to the hospital struck him as almost miraculous.

David harbored his own set of fears, but they had nothing to do with the state of Aruba's medical care or the inconveniences of island life. David worried about Bula failing. A shot of dread went through him whenever he imagined they might have to shutter the shop.

"Those were agonizing moments," David confided. "I didn't want to waste the rest of my life writing legal briefs."

A couple days after his scary trip to the ER, David was back surfing.

"One thing that kept me going, whenever something was frustrating or a pain in the ass, was the thought I couldn't give up," he said. "There was no way in hell I was going to be the guy running a surf shop who didn't surf."

When I interviewed David about his early passion for surfing, I had hoped for something with lots of sizzle and drama. After all, surfing is the embodiment of everything cool, a sport associated with extreme athleticism, risk, and hedonistic abandon. So it took me aback when David compared his development as a surfer to the same approach he uses when testing a new recipe—as a series of tiny improvements and adjustments.

"Sorry, I never had a big graduation moment as a surfer," he said, almost apologetically.

His comment strikes at the heart of a subversive myth about following a passion. In 2005, Steve Jobs gave a famous commencement speech at Stanford University about loving what you do. Don't settle for anything less than work you love, he warned. "The only way to do great work," he said, "is to love what you do."

"Follow your passion" may make an inspiring slogan, but I believe it has harmful implications in the real world. The phrase implies there's an alternative universe where your passion sits like a shiny new car on the lot. You just have to poke around and pick it out. Once you've made your choice, you can expect instant nirvana. According to the passion myth, it's a case of love at first sight. You and your passion ride off into the sunset, happily ever after.

This is such a romantic mindset, but dangerously unrealistic. The early stages of mastering anything of value might not feel fantastic at all. As surfers say, surfing boils down to inventing new ways to fail. Learning to surf requires you to put up with your own incompetence long enough to reap the benefits. If you stick with it long enough, you can identify and eventually overcome your weak points. The bouts of frustration—of getting sucked down into an underwater mosh pit like a hapless guppy—aren't easily overcome, except by trial . . . and more error.

"Following your passion is a luxury. Following your values is a necessity. Passion is a fickle magnet: it pulls you toward your current interests. Values are a steady compass: they point you toward a future purpose." [14]

ADAM GRANT, ORGANIZATIONAL PSYCHOLOGIST
AT THE WHARTON SCHOOL

The passion creed suggests that if something isn't immediately enjoyable, it doesn't qualify as a true calling. That's bullshit. Passion is mutable, rising and falling like barometric pressure.

Terri Trespicio, author of *Unfollow Your Passion: How to Create a Life that Matters to You,* debunks the follow-your-passion catchphrase. Passion is not a plan, she tells us. It's a feeling, and feelings change. "Rather than stand outside with a bucket waiting for it to rain," she writes, "you need to set up the pipes and get the water moving through them so you have it on demand." [15]

Trespicio advises we should hunker down and get to work, even when we don't know where our efforts will lead us. As she points out, the Karate Kid spent countless days waxing Mr. Miyagi's car and painting his fence, only to discover later that he'd built up a repertoire of skills essential to mastering a complex discipline. He didn't magically follow a prepackaged passion. He *developed* it, over time, in the small moments.

In my mind, David is the Karate Kid of surfing. Even when he got battered by his own ineptitude, he kept showing up. His grittiness counted for a lot in Aruba's insular surfing community. Gradually, almost imperceptibly, David built up his skills and confidence. The better he got, the more he wanted to head out into the chop, with waves coming in as fast as he could count them.

Both he and Yair possessed that doggedness and patience for making small improvements. They threw themselves at the challenge of running a small business, knowing they would sometimes fail spectacularly. Consciously or not, David and Yair practiced John C. Maxwell's famous philosophy: "Fail early, fail often, but always fail forward." Failing forward is all about risking failure within a small and controlled scope of impact, to achieve eventual success.

> *"Well-being is realized by small steps,*
> *but [that] is truly no small thing."*
>
> ZENO, PHILOSOPHER, PHYSICIAN,
> AND FOUNDER OF STOICISM

I've never ridden a surfboard, either standing or lying down. But I can picture David and Yair paddling out into Aruba's wild surf, driven by the same dream of slicing across the whitewash and sending up a lacy trail of spray. Bobbing on their boards, getting thrown around by a rough sea, they probably didn't look like entrepreneurs hell-bent on pursuing a passion. But now I know: There's no thrill without the patience of staring at the ocean, waiting for the next good wave. Because as surfing reminds us, it's rarely the big showy moves that explain our success. It's the smallest ones, repeated faithfully over time. Small things, as Zeno observed, are truly no small thing. They add up, multiply, and compound.

"Luck Has Nothing to Do With It"

Yair: Surfing is the absolute epitome of small, imperceptible improvements. Like, 80 percent of whether you get a good ride is how well you position yourself in the lineup. That's something that comes with years and years of being in the water. You basically have to just bob around like a cork and look at the waves. Little by little your mind learns to recognize where the wave will start breaking or if it will close out, in which case you don't want to take it. Wave knowledge is kind of an impossible thing to teach.

You don't even realize you're getting better at it until you stop and reflect: Now you can glance at a wave coming in and predict how it will break, super fast or slower, and in a certain direction.

David: It took me several sessions before I was even able to sit on the board—I kept falling off in the chop. I'd made a classic rookie mistake: I grossly underestimated the level of difficulty.

Yair: People watching a group of surfers from the beach might say, "Look at that guy . . . he always seems to be in the right place at the right time. He's so lucky." Luck has nothing to do with it. That guy knows exactly where the wave is going to break. We're talking about a tiny difference of three feet to the right or left. It's being able to position yourself and angle your board perfectly.

David: It took me weeks and weeks to do anything even halfway competent. Even getting up on the board and riding a small wave took me forever. I'm not a gifted athlete. Yair's the jock. I'm much more the lily-livered sissy. It's just understood he will perform better in any sport. And to this day, twenty years later, I've never had a moment as a surfer when I thought, *Okay, I got this.*

A Short Break for Surf Slang[16]

The language of surfing is a lot more complex and nuanced than you might think. You can't just get by on a handful of buzzwords. It's like any language. If you know just a few words and overuse them, you brand yourself as a clueless tourist.

As far back as the 1920s, surfers invented or repurposed words as an insider means of expressing themselves. Back then, Waikiki surfers eyed the horizon for bluebirds (big waves), avoided the soup (whitewater), and maneuvered to keep their big wooden boards from sliding ass (losing tail-end traction).

A subset of surf slang wound its way into popular culture over the years, including "wipeout," "stoked" (thrilled or excited), "grom" (young surfer), and "jams" (long loose-fitting trunks). Surfing words that make it into common usage often do so after losing their coolness among core surfers. A character in a 1950s "Howdy Doody Show" originally used the made-up word *Kowa-bunga!* to voice shock or surprise. Southern California surfers grabbed the word, changed its spelling, and adopted it as their own.

Soon the entertainment world stole the word back. In a 1965 cartoon, Snoopy of Peanuts fame yells *Cowabunga!* as he rides a wave. The expression got picked up in the '80s by the cartoon characters Teenage Mutant Ninja Turtles and, later, by Bart Simpson. As surf expressions crept inland, adopted by nonsurfing couch potatoes, they lost popularity in surfing circles. Using words like "cowabunga," "rad," and "dweeb" became the opposite of hip.

It's treacherous business, trying to sound cool in the surfing world. As a nonsurfer, you're bound to sound lame or dated, like someone who still uses expressions like "groovy, man" and "peachy keen" around young people.

"The problem is that youth culture is a moving target," David warned me. "Almost anything you write will get eye rolls."

He's right, of course. I completely misjudged the difficulty of writing about a topic as complex and unpredictable as surf slang. My takeaway: Surf lingo, like any living language, is like a parade, always moving and morphing. Any attempt at pinning it down is futile. And that's exactly what makes it so cool.

10

Purple Cow-ing It

After school, a knot of skateboarders gathered in front of Bula's storefront. Inside, David and Yair concentrated on their latest time suck, a new light fixture with mismatched parts. The air-conditioning had petered out, and it was blazing hot in the shop. When David and Yair looked up from their task, they saw a row of pimply faces smashed against the front window.

Yair went outside and greeted the kids. He wiped sweat off his face with the hem of his T-shirt.

"No, we're not ready to open yet." He glanced back at the shop. "Come back on Monday."

He recognized a couple of the skateboarders, two brothers. They lived in a small house the color of desert sand with potted flowers on the windowsill. Two aloe plants flanked their front door, symbols of good luck and prosperity. In the densely packed neighborhood where the brothers lived, news traveled with rocket speed from one house to the next.

David and Yair now faced another obstacle—how to block the view of the chaos inside the shop from curious passersby. With no money or time for fancy signage, they sat down on the shop floor and started tossing ideas back and forth. "We were good about brainstorming," David later told me. "It was a case of groping in the dark with no flashlight, but eventually we'd come up with something useful."

The morning after their brainstorm, David and Yair gathered up their stash of surfing magazines and brought them into the shop. They moved fast, ripping out pages and taping them up on the front window in no particular order. Soon, they had covered the storefront with a montage of colorful photos and stories. Shirtless surfers carried gleaming boards to the water's edge. Trenches of thick blue sea rolled toward a crescent beach. A lone figure in a wetsuit knifed across the face of a sunlit wave.

The most artful photos came from *The Surfer's Journal*, the *National Geographic* of surfing magazines. David and Yair loved its silken, glossy pages and lingered over the profiles. One issue featured Wayne Lynch, an Australian surfing legend, riding an angry sea on a yellow surfboard. On the facing page, another surfing hero crouched low, arms pointing to the heavens, as he glided across a glassy ten-foot wave. A photographer had taken the photos in Fiji as a howling trade wind thrashed the seas. His slow-motion camera technique gave all the photos a raw, soulful mood.

That was exactly the mood David and Yair imagined for Bula.

Theirs was a simple, ingenious idea: Hide Bula behind a wall of surfers' dreams while finishing the renovations. It's difficult to overestimate the passion and loyalty that surf magazines inspired back then. California surf writer Sam George compared surf magazines to the Koran, the Book of Tao, and the Bible as the printed means of reaffirming the "faith in a philosophy, a way of life. The only difference is that [surf magazines] come out monthly."[17]

Soon the underground buzz about Bula's opening spread across the island. Middle schoolers and teenagers paused in front of the shop, checking out the images of surfers gliding across walls of majestic waves. They pictured themselves riding the invisible energy of those same storm-generated waves—the perfect turns, cutbacks, and aerials. At school, Bula's future customers doodled pictures of surfboards in the margins of their class notes. The anticipation of Aruba's first legit surf shop, with skateboards and cool gear, was almost too much to bear.

Most of the words we read without realizing it—signs and billboards, advertisements on the sides of buses and trains, magazine covers at newsstands, and millions of online pop-ups—are foisted on us by marketers. Maybe their advertising ploys catch our attention for a split second, but we quickly tune out. The words and images bore us. Worse, they're intrusive, and a waste of our precious time.

Let's compare these time wasters with the stories we willingly want to read. Maybe we find them in a favorite book or magazine. Our cherished stories reflect and engage the whole of our attention, not just fragments engineered for an advertiser's profit. The best of them take us to a special interior place where we can dream, soothe our spirits, and learn about the world.

Rather than taking the traditional marketing route, David and Yair climbed inside the heads of their potential customers and intuited what they might actually want to see or read. They invited their future customers to linger in front of the shop, not with a clever headline or artfully designed window display, but with stories and photos ripped from surfing magazines. Their approach cost nothing, yet it was remarkably effective.

When David and Yair first told me about their magazine wall, I didn't think much of the idea. I pictured a ragtag collection of pages held together by ugly strips of tape. As a marketing snob, steeped in corporate branding, I wanted to roll my eyes and say, *"Really?"*

Plastering old magazines across a storefront struck me as way too slapdash for a new retail shop trying to establish itself. "You only get one chance to make a first impression" floated into my mind and almost out of my mouth. If they had asked for my advice, I would have put on my brand bonnet and droned on about the importance of brand attributes, unique selling propositions, and professionally designed graphics. But thank goodness, they didn't ask.

"Bootstrapping entrepreneurs often upend existing industries because the dominant players in an industry are the last places you'll find empowered mavericks."[18]

—SETH GODIN, BUSINESS PUNDIT AND
BESTSELLING AUTHOR

Traditional marketing might have worked for a new hotel chain or larger retailer, but not for Bula. Rather than blending into the retail environment, David and Yair took a Purple Cow approach. According to Seth Godin, Purple Cow entrepreneurs tell stories so intriguing, people want to stop, pay attention, and spread the word. Godin calls these contagious ideas "ideaviruses." They're carried by "sneezers," his fun term for the super-spreaders who love to blab to their friends about a new product or service. Every market has a few sneezers. Intriguing them is the essential first step to achieving Purple Cow status.

Bula's original sneezers were sweaty skateboarders and hardcore surfers, a fringe market in Aruba. That's another Purple Cow principle: Target a niche instead of the masses. Identify an underserved slice of the mainstream, and give them something to care about. If your chosen niche is tightly knit, the ideas will spread faster. According to Godin, that's how innovators cross the chasm from boring and safe to remarkable.

11

Bubble, Bubble, Toil, and Trouble

Yair and David scrambled to finish the wallpaper in time for Bula's opening day. It was getting dark, and they were ravenous. All day, they'd been ticking items off their list, with a short midday break for lunch from a nearby food truck. Amid all the uncertainties of starting a retail business, they figured they could knock off the wallpapering project in no time.

The wallpaper design, Polynesian palm trees, looked great on Bula's dingy melamine panels. The swaying palms infused the shop with a tropical vibe prized in Aruba. Contrary to popular belief, palm trees aren't a common sight in most of Aruba. Unlike other Caribbean islands, with their lush green vegetation, Aruba's landscapes specialize in sandy stretches of desert, sculpted rock formations, and huge diorite boulders.

Across the island, several species of cactus jut from the sand and rock, defying the strong winds. Locals use the cactus for livestock fences, in soups, and even as Christmas decorations. Spiky aloe plants grow in abundance, as do over fifty species of fruit trees. On their walks home from school, local kids pilfer the tastier fruits—aromatic mangoes, the tart Aruban cherry, guava, and soursop—growing wild in their neighbors' yards.

Tourists have to travel to Aruba's ritzy resorts to luxuriate in classic Caribbean-style landscaping. Along the western coastline, the high-end hotels showcase tropical trees, plants, and flowers: allamanda, manila palm, coconut palm, hibiscus, poinsettia, oleander, and frangipani. The exotic specimens arrive in huge container ships and get transplanted with care into Aruba's arid soil. The hotels work hard to create an illusion of a lunar-desert-meets-tropical paradise.

Aruba's known for its ancient rock formations like the ones you see at Ayo and Casibari. Photo credit: Paula Costa, dreamstime.com.

The verdant resort landscapes offer a striking contrast to Aruba's vast stretches of desert. Photo credit: Redtango, dreamstime.com.

Wallpaper palms served as Bula's self-made version of a tropical paradise. Right away, though, David and Yair ran into problems measuring, cutting, and matching up serrated branches and leaves.

David got fixated on an issue with the gluing. The flaw in one section was so minor, customers would never have noticed. But under the stress of preparing for opening day, the imperfection struck David as a looming crisis. Exasperated, he put down his roller and argued for using more brute force when smoothing out the glue. Yair listened and jumped in with his own idea for a fix: Let the wet sheet relax for at least five minutes while preparing the next one. The tension built between them.

The Great Glue Debate was emblematic of their relationship at the time: Each wanted to prove the other one wrong, or at least less right. Under pressure, David reverted to his law school training. In mock trials, his law professors gave him top marks for his persistence. He always dug deeper to defend a position, even when he knew he'd lost the argument.

Adam Grant, an organizational psychologist at the Wharton School, has studied obstinacy and why so many of us find it difficult to back off from our own views. In his book *Think Again: The Power of Knowing What You Don't Know*, he identifies three modes of defending our positions. Preachers argue their beliefs by saying, "Look, I've found the answer. My job is to proselytize a sacred truth." Prosecutors reverse the logic, saying, "My job is to prove you wrong, and I'll show you all the reasons I'm right." The third type, politicians, cherish their popularity and crave people's approval, even if that means adjusting the facts: "My job is to get people on my side, no matter what it takes."

David argued for his wallpaper fix with the instincts of a well-trained prosecutor. By nature, Yair was more mellow, but he, too, liked to win. Yair may have had a bit of the righteous preacher in him when he suggested they let the wet wallpaper sheets relax before gluing them to the wall. When tensions escalated to the breaking point, they retreated to their corners.

They told me about the wallpaper debacle on a Zoom call one Sunday evening. I could see Yair struggling to get comfortable on the sofa. He cradled his head on a pillow and chimed in less than usual. David covered for him, reminding me of Yair's usual Sunday schedule. He gets up before dawn, fishes all day, and brings home fresh catch for dinner. Yair had had a good haul that Sunday: two large Ziplocks of wahoo and mahi-mahi filets, fresh from the sea. He grew up fishing the steep and chaotic seas off Aruba's southern shores. The waves come rushing around the southern tip of the island, creating a maelstrom of crosscurrents and choppy seas. The fishing is especially good in the currents, but Yair and his boat always take a beating.

I admit I felt a mixture of relief and curiosity when David and Yair told me they'd argued about the wallpaper. What friends don't get ticked at each other? After several months of interviews, David and Yair had never once shown even a hint of irritation toward each other. That didn't seem normal to me.

On the day of the wallpaper incident, they told me that they didn't let the tension escalate or get catty. Apparently, they stayed mad at each other for a while, then pretended the spat had never happened.

"As in a marriage, if the other person is kinda wrong—and both people realize it—then one will back off," said Yair. "The secret is silent resentment."

Yair quickly added, with a smile, "But I don't want to go down in history as the Silent Resentment Guy."

Yair's comment got me thinking. Therapists advise couples never to let the sun go down on an argument. Yair and David ignored that advice. They essentially put wallpaper over a leaky pipe and didn't look back. To make sense of their mode of resolving the conflict, I spoke with Elana Kupor, LMHC, who has a private therapy practice in Seattle, Washington.

"Often a fight is about something else," she told me. "Couples may argue about where to put the spatula, but often they're upset about something deeper." She doubts David and Yair were all that concerned about the bubbles or their amateur wallpapering attempts. Maybe they were worried the wallpaper fiasco was an omen about Bula's slim chances of succeeding. Or maybe they felt out of their depth about their ability to run a business, together or apart. All the pressures were there, bubbling in the moment. When you add in their exhaustion and hunger, it's no wonder they got riled up and then retreated without saying a word.

"Good friends don't always have to talk through a conflict if they can let it go," Kupor observed. "Sometimes a fight is just a passing reaction to a stressful trigger." Neither Yair nor David cared all that much about the wallpaper, so they let the tempest blow over with no lasting damage. Their détente strikes me as a smart, practical solution. There was just so much at stake in preserving their friendship. After they got a little perspective, and maybe something to eat, they were able to shrug off the conflict.

I've thought a lot about the infamous wallpapering conflict, and this is what I now believe: Ideally, we can understand and accept when our friends occasionally act out, just as parents accept that their children are flawed creatures. Most parents don't blame their toddlers when they scream, pound the table, or spill their milk. They don't expect their kids to be perfect. The same holds true for best friends. We can witness each other's flaws with tenderness and acceptance. That's the essence of a great friendship. Even more, it's a form of love.

Reflecting back, both David and Yair are fuzzy on how they wrapped up the wallpaper project. "I'm pretty sure his solution was better," admitted David. "When confronted by my own ineptitude, I acted like a total brat."

Both of them vividly remember the next hurdle: dealing with the Ts, boardshorts, and bikinis they had hauled back in duffels from Coconut Grove. The clothes were wrinkled almost past recognition. Debbie and Ana came to the rescue with steamers and smoothed out the fabric. They all pitched in with ideas about how to display the merchandise on the racks and shelves: the women's shorts here, the men's shorts there, and the bikinis by the changing rooms.

When they finished putting out the clothes, Bula still looked a little malnourished, like a store after a big closeout sale. At least the wallpaper and Yair's racks added charm to the space. Yair had turned random scraps of driftwood into end pieces with drilled holes for the plumber pipe, Bula's version of a hanging rack for clothes. He suspended the six racks with manila ropes. The overall effect registered as mellow and organic. Total cost: $40. It was a point of pride they hadn't depleted their meager start-up reserves on pricey retail fixtures.

In time, the hanging racks would become an iconic feature of Bula. For now, David and Yair just hoped they'd attract enough buyers to keep the store open. It was April 5, 2003, just two days before Bula's official opening.

Dawn Patrol

On This Day: April 7, 2003
#1 Song in the United States: "In Da Club" by 50 Cent
65th NCAA Basketball Championship: Syracuse beats Kansas, 81–78
U.S. troops capture Baghdad

April 7, 2003, Oranjestad, Aruba—Yair Lichtenstein and David Putnam, an American, announce the opening of Bula Surf Shop in the Royal Plaza Mall. To mark the occasion, they drove at dawn to Wariruri Cove. The shop owners arrived with a fresh batch of savory pastechis, Aruba's favorite fast food. They brought enough golden-fried pastries to share with the other surfers on dawn patrol.

With twenty-four-mile-per-hour winds out of the east, David caught a nice right, nailed his bottom turn, and did a competent cutback. A friendly nearby surfer shouted "*Dushi yiu!*" as David paddled back out into the lineup.

"It wasn't an incredible wave," David said. "But I was stoked by the warm welcome the locals gave me."

Around 7:30 a.m., David and Yair paddled back to shore. They had only two hours to get the shop ready for opening day. As they approached the beach, a frigate bird swooped down from the shore. The man-o-war has a forked tail and the largest wingspan-to-body-weight ratio of any bird. Half-napping, half-alert, the tropical seabird can stay aloft on wind currents for more than a week.

As David and Yair watched, the bird grabbed a small silvery fish out of the water and flapped his wings toward the rising sun.

"We took that as a lucky omen for Bula's future," Yair said. He shouted a cheerful good morning—*bon dia*—to a couple of "latecomers" who just arrived at the surf break. David and Yair loaded up their boards and washed the sand off their feet with water out of a jug stowed in the truck.

"Dawn patrol was a ceremonial occasion for us," David said. "It reminded us of the reason we wanted to open a surf shop."

An Exercise in Minimalism

When David and Yair stepped onto the slowpoke escalator at the Royal Plaza, they had sand between their toes, sea salt on their skin, and crispy "surfer hair." David and Yair came by the sexy, wind-blown look naturally. They'd simply made a beeline to Bula Surf Shop after dawn patrol at Wariruri.

It was 8:30 a.m. on Monday, April 7, 2003, just sixty minutes until Bula's birth. Outwardly, they were in good spirits, a couple of young kids on Christmas morning. They'd worked hard to arrive at this moment of truth. "We'd run into nonstop challenges, mostly due to our own incompetence," David told me. "We were just a couple of decently educated guys fumbling to learn the ropes of retail."

Both of them had a touch of nerves. Although they weren't superstitious, the morning headlines about U.S. troops capturing Baghdad had put a damper on their mood. What if the bottom fell out of the world economy? The threat of global unrest amplified their own private worries about Bula's chances of making it. They had no way of knowing if zero, five, or fifty people would show up.

With scant financial reserves, they'd opted for a minimalist launch. No ads, hype, or hoopla. Maybe they were spooked by the research they'd read: Couples who stage a lavish wedding exponentially increase their chances of getting divorced. David and Yair didn't want that dismal fate for Bula. Plus, they were atrocious self-promoters, with lowball expectations. If they managed to keep the doors open and pay the bills, that would be their idea of nirvana.

They busied themselves with mindless tasks. Yair spread out a few T-shirts hanging on a rack to create the illusion of having more merchandise. David popped a VHS surfing reel into each of the clunky television monitors over the two changing rooms. Then he slid a CD into his laptop hooked up with speakers. To set the mood, he chose his go-to rapper in 2003, Dr. Octagon.

At the stroke of 9:30, David and Yair opened the door. It thrilled them to see a small milling crowd of locals, mostly skaters cradling skateboards under their arms. Yair motioned them inside with a cheerful greeting: *Bon dia! Pasa nu ma ruman.* "Good morning! Come on in, brother."

They recognized many of the faces. Mandy, a sixteen-year-old, had waited weeks, with growing impatience, for the day Bula opened for business. She was one of the skimboarders who'd scoped out the shop when David and Yair first taped the magazine montage on the front window. She scooted around the store, gathering outfits and trying them on in a changing room. After a lengthy deliberation, she put down $10 on layaway for a denim skirt from the Rusty apparel line. As Bula's first official paying customer, she got a double fist bump and proudly left the store carrying her receipt in a blue Bula bag.

Throughout the rest of the day, people drifted in and out of the shop. The middle schoolers raced to the display of skateboards, fondling them like sacred relics. With their meager allowance, Bula's earliest fans had just enough to buy a few stickers (about $1.70 each) to decorate their beat-up boards. They'd plant themselves in front of the glass case, agonizing whether to buy the sticker of the cows mating, an artist's rendering of a steaming pile of poop, or a fireball crushing the earth.

Other than ringing up stickers, Mandy's layaway, and a few other sales, the cash register got little use that first day.

"It Was More Like a Backyard Party . . . and Then People Started Buying Stuff"

David: The night before we opened, it occurred to us that we didn't know how to use a cash register. How dumb is that? I remember thinking, *Oh, this is how they do it at Taco Bell.*

Yair: I didn't expect much on our first day. It surprised me every time someone walked through the door.

David: Your mother stopped by and gave us a really nice plant.

Yair: It was more like a backyard party . . . and then people started buying stuff.

David: I got an existential thrill every time I rang someone up and handed them change.

Yair: Yeah, me too. And I remember Mandy, our very first customer, checked out everything we had in women's clothing—the bikinis, sundresses, and a few other pieces. And when she picked out the Rusty jean skirt, it felt extra sweet because Rusty was the only brand [at Surf Expo] that hadn't treated us like a total waste of time.

David: We should have been a lot more stressed than we were. Our ignorance of our ignorance gave us a false sense of security.

Yair: It's amazing, really, that we sold a decent amount. Today we would consider April 7 a terrible day, but we saw a couple hundred dollars.

David: There was a Dunning-Kruger aspect to it . . . that blind spot of underestimating our incompetence.

Yair: Well, the bar we set was pretty low, right? Our dream was to make a sustainable business that, you know, wouldn't go bankrupt right away. Low expectations, maybe *that* was our secret. We never wanted to aim so high that we'd have a long way to fall. We were always bracing for the worst, which made us inordinately happy when something good happened. That weird combination of pessimism and naivete worked in our favor.

13

Twilight Zone

From Day One, the same driftwood sign has hung on Bula's front door. One side shouts a friendly GONE SURFING in blocky, hand-painted blue letters. Flip it, and the letters spell OPEN.

The sign was an Ana creation. She made it from a piece of wood that had washed up at Wariruri.

"We considered it a lucky talisman to have wood from our favorite beach hanging on the door," David told me.

At a craft store, Ana found paint that matched Bula's signature blue shopping bags. Her brushwork struck a nice balance between "I made this myself" and artistic. When she finished, she showed the sign to Yair. He showed his appreciation by lifting her off the ground in an enveloping bear hug. Then he got his drill and bored two holes for the rope loop.

Presto, Bula had its very own welcoming sign.

Each morning David and Yair flipped the sign to OPEN and wondered: *Is this the day we'll sell nothing at all?*

For long stretches, no paying customers came into the shop. As the minutes ticked by, they sat side by side at the cash bar, white-knuckling it. To pass the time, they surfed the internet and updated Bula's web page, which was a pre–social media gallery that celebrated local wave riders with photo albums of their aquatic exploits. The online attention gave the locals a shot in the arm. They got pumped up looking at themselves online, reliving the moment they rode a wave, any wave—big, small, perfectly peeling, or blown-out slop.

"Those three things—autonomy, complexity, and a connection between reward and effort—are, most people agree, the three qualities that work has to have if it is to be satisfying."[19]

MALCOLM GLADWELL, BESTSELLING
AUTHOR AND PODCAST HOST

At closing time, David and Yair went through the ritual of updating their scorecard, a spreadsheet of sales estimates compared to actuals. The grim tally rarely came close to their naively optimistic projections. They'd boost their spirits by reminding each other of the misery of the careers they'd left behind. Even on Bula's worst days, they wore their self-reliance proudly. They were safe from micromanaging bosses and smug academics. No one was breathing down their necks. The freedom and autonomy felt exhilarating, a sweet reward for their previous suffering.

When the waves were especially good, no one would have blamed them if they had said, "Fuck it," and quit early. It was a simple matter of turning off the lights, locking the door, and flipping the sign to the other side. A couple of times they may have left a few minutes early—they don't exactly remember—but the Gone Surfing temptation never developed into a bad habit. As best friends and entrepreneurs, they had pledged to give Bula an honorable, fighting chance. Surf shop owners already had a bad enough reputation as slackers and flakes; they refused to reinforce the stereotype.

In quiet moments, David and Yair added new tracks to their ever-evolving Bula playlist. They were huge music fans with similar eccentric tastes in bands. One of their early favorites was Modest Mouse, an indie rock band from the West Coast. True to its name, Modest Mouse had a moody, unpolished sound. One critic gave its 2000 release, "The Moon & Antarctica," muted praise as the "weirdest yet . . . cohesive, if flawed." David and Yair admired the band's reprobate coolness and love of experimental sounds, even at the expense of commercial success.

The band fit the Bula ethos to a T. David and Yair envisioned Bula as a democratic community experiment, what the sociologists call a "third space," not just a place for selling merchandise.

At first, they wanted to squeeze in a sofa where customers could chill. But there was no room in the tiny shop. So they cleared a spot for a narrow blue bench. That's where the skateboarders perched. After skateboarding at the nearby park, hordes of sweaty preadolescent kids descended on the shop. The middle schoolers cooled down in the air-conditioning, watched surfing movies, and swapped lies about various tricks they claimed to have landed. Rarely did they buy anything. Bula was their living room.

Bula's informal, laid-back atmosphere was unheard of in Aruba where retailers had an old-fashioned, often formal, approach to customer service. Yair compared it to the original Woolworth's in New York with ladies in uniforms and gloves. He went on to say that "scruffy" lower-income Arubans invariably got the cold shoulder. Younger people, too.

"So we didn't want to be jerks and just kick them out," Yair told me.

One afternoon a well-dressed Venezuelan woman with a young daughter walked into Bula carrying a Louis Vuitton shopping bag. She glanced around the store and fixated on the display of expensive sunglasses. Just then a group of skaters burst through the door and gathered in front of the display, blocking her view. A look of contempt flashed across her face as if to say, *I'm far too refined and wealthy to be in this place.*

She flounced out, dragging her daughter behind her. Over the next few weeks, the same scenario repeated itself a dozen times. David and Yair lavished attention on the hard-core surfers and skaters—customers marginalized by other retailers—and let the tourists fend for themselves. It was their way of signaling their legitimacy as new surf-shop owners.

"We didn't know how to prioritize our service," explained Yair when I asked about their approach. "Even when a big fish was swimming in our midst, we kind of ignored it."

A few months after Bula opened, Yair traveled overseas to get medical care for a flare-up of Crohn's disease. David was left tending the shop without him. That's when the shop had its most abysmal day on record. Without Yair's steadying influence, waves of panic washed over David.

"It was just so insanely quiet, a twilight zone, " he recalled. "I almost couldn't make sense of it." He felt a little screwed up in his head, missing his friend and worrying about the future.

As soon as Yair returned to Aruba, they pulled into their usual parking spaces behind the Royal Plaza earlier than usual. On the way, they'd each fantasized, but only briefly, about the waves they hadn't been able to ride that morning. It was almost comically sunny, and the sea shone with a bright green-blue hue neither Pantone nor Crayola could possibly replicate.

Yair arrived with two smoothies—a mind-clearing blend of kiwi, coconut, and lime juice—and took his usual seat at the cash bar next to David. They talked about Bula, their tiny sinking boat. On paper, the shop was breaking even, but barely. They knew the business wouldn't pull through unless something changed.

"It didn't take a genius to figure out that the sweaty skateboarders wouldn't help us pay rent or salaries," David explained to me. "Worse, the customers with money didn't want to be around hordes of young kids."

Uncurbed idealism had lured them into a trap. They needed a new blueprint, one grounded in more realistic expectations. After spitballing a few ideas and discarding the bad ones, the puzzle pieces came together in a flash of insight. In retrospect, it seemed so obvious. They couldn't believe they hadn't thought of it sooner. For Bula's survival, they would need to line up all three legs of the authenticity stool: *community spirit + cool products + the right customers.*

The next day they hauled away the blue bench and dismantled the skateboard displays. Over the next few weeks, the onslaught of skateboarders thinned. Most of them found somewhere else to go after school. If anyone asked about the change, David and Yair gave the identical answer. It wasn't fair to the community, they said, to sell skateboards if they didn't skate.

"Sure, it was a little bit of a party line," admitted David, "but we didn't want to hurt anyone's feelings."

The truth was they'd decided to focus on what they loved, surfing. Every time they said it, they got more buoyed and optimistic about Bula's future. They were only a few months into their experiment. There was plenty of time to tinker with the recipe for success. The near misses and wipeouts were all part of it, just like in surfing.

Bula finally weathered its first few months thanks in part to a competitor's misfortune. Aruba's most successful beach shop, Bula's chief rival, went bust. Apparently, the owner was swimming in personal debt. It was pure luck he went out of business when he did. Now there was nowhere else to go for fashionable beachwear. Overnight, Bula was the only game in town.

When David told me about that sad slow day he sat in the shop, missing Yair and worrying about Bula's future, I remembered a famous friendship study. Researchers placed students wearing heavy backpacks at the base of a hill and asked them to estimate its steepness. Participants who stood next to a friend gave lower estimates of the incline than those who were alone. Conversely, when subjects were asked to think of a person they disliked, they estimated the hill as even more steep.

The lead researcher for the study at the University of Virginia, Dr. Dennis Proffitt, concluded that the students in the study assessed life differently when a friend was nearby. "They find the hill to be steeper if they are alone, and less so if they are with friends." The study also concludes that the more time participants spent with a friend, the shallower the hill appeared.[20]

Let that sink in for a minute. We all suspect that good friends make us feel good and more confident. Now scientists have proof. When confronted with challenges that might otherwise seem overwhelming, people with a support system can slip into another gear that motivates them to think, *Okay, I'm still going to try to climb this.* Next to a friend, higher and steeper doesn't mean impossible. But if we let ourselves dwell on someone we don't like, we perceive the hill as a slog and a stressor to avoid.

A related study highlighted MRI brain activity when a subject received mild, intermittent electrical shocks while alone or while holding a friend's hand. The research concluded that our anticipatory anxiety, the type of stress so many of us live with, lessens when we held the hand of a friend.[21] The friend's presence actually calms our brain waves and reduces our anxiety.

Where am I going with all this?

First, the warm-and-fuzzy topic of friendship has found its way into the realm of rigorous scientific study, and I'm grateful for that. Scientists invite us to consider the significance of our friendships for our psychological and physical well-being. The consensus: The topic of friendship deserves its own spot alongside "eat your veggies, exercise, and get enough sleep."

Second, I suspect David felt worse about Bula's chances of making it when he was alone in the shop, with no metaphoric hand to hold. Contrast that with the later scene of the two of them sitting in their two-man strategic huddle, swilling fruit smoothies. They lifted each other up. Their brain waves quieted and got in sync, like the rare moment when a wave angle coincides with the perfect wind conditions. The power magnifies. When you click with someone, because you have shared interests and enjoy each other, it's pure magic.

"Thank God, Our Overhead Was So Low"

David: I don't remember us caving into the temptation to quit and go surfing.

Yair: Yeah, well, at first, we may have left a little early some days, right? On a good day, we'd think, *Well, we already made some money, why stick around?* Dumb! If we had a great day, that's when we needed to stick around and capitalize on that.

David: Okay, now I remember that super slow day we said, *screw it,* and closed up early.

Yair: One of us, I don't remember who [laughter], forgot to lock up. We got out of the water around 7:30 p.m., and there were, like, a hundred missed calls on my phone. We rushed back and saw a security guard, keeping customers away. We felt like bozos.

David: I remember how easily we got rattled back then.

Yair: Those early days were tough, mentally. Thank god, our overhead was so low.

David: It sounds corny, but I remember thinking that, if Bula was going to drown in the retail bankruptcy seas, at least I'd have my best friend by my side.

14

Side by Side

When David and Yair told me they used to sit side by side, day after day, working on Bula's homegrown website, I couldn't get the image out of my mind. The scene so perfectly conforms to the classic gender archetype: two guy friends hanging out, not talking about anything deep or profound, just getting stuff done.

The stereotypical gender differences in friendship styles both fascinate and baffle me. The next time you're at a gathering, check out the same-sex pairs engaged in conversation. You'll probably notice women tend to face each other, looking directly into each other's eyes, while men often stand at an angle of about 120 degrees, shoulder to shoulder. As the friendship expert Robin Dunbar notes, men are perfectly capable of standing face to face. When they're talking to women, they often will. But it appears they find looking at another man's eyes disconcerting, like a caveman threat, so they angle their bodies away from each other.[22]

Dunbar and other friendship experts use the phrase "side by side" or "shoulder to shoulder" to highlight a certain lack of demonstrable intimacy between male friends. According to the archetype, men bond over something they can watch or engage in, preferably a rugged virile sport.

Women, the research tells us, are more likely to gaze directly at each other over a glass of Pinot Grigio or cup of tea. Typical women friends exchange emotional intel and secrets while demonstrating their support for each other. By contrast, male friendships seem to thrive on physical activity, good-hearted ridicule, and outlandish rituals. These broad gender comparisons help explain why a group of guys can watch the Super Bowl, year after year, and not know how many kids a friend has or whether a buddy's marriage is crumbling.

According to Geoffrey L. Greif, professor at the University of Maryland and author of *Buddy System: Understanding Male Friendships,* many men don't think deeply about their friendships or make them a priority. They may even avoid talking about them. Greif told me that he believes the reticence may have something to do with the American spirit of rugged individualism: Rely on yourself and not others, and don't get too close to men who might be competitors.

In interviews with hundreds of people, Greif reported another deep-seated concern. A quarter of the men he spoke to worried aloud about coming across as gay. Apparently, the adolescent fear of being mocked for getting too close to another guy travels into adulthood for many men. The cultural message: Don't express your emotions or show vulnerability in a conventionally feminine way. That cultural bias has contributed to the epidemic rise of male loneliness in midlife and beyond.[23]

Knowing this makes me incredibly sad. Don't we all need the primal connections, trust, and acceptance of our friends? Men should have the right to intimate friendships if they choose. Equally, women need their casual, occasional buddies.

If you'll allow me to get up on a soapbox here, I want to give a shout-out to David and Yair. When I look at their early friendship, I see all the usual sporting activities, gestures of loyalty, in-jokes, mockery, and bravado of young men. I also see an unwavering commitment. The Japanese use the word *nakama* to identify a best friend, a close buddy, or someone for whom we feel true nonromantic love. More than a mere friend, this person is someone who's embedded in our emotional life—a serious connection, not available or possible for everyone.

David and Yair are examples of straight guys whose friendship doesn't threaten nor diminish their manliness. The term "bromance" aptly describes their relationship. A skating magazine in the 1990s coined the word to describe dudes who often skate together. As with any strong cultural trend, Hollywood embraced it. Brad Pitt and George Clooney are bromantic, as are Matt Damon and Ben Affleck, Owen Wilson and Ben Stiller, Hugh Laurie and Stephen Fry. These celebrity friends work together, socialize, and say glowing things about each other.

It's fun to imagine them offstage in their natural habitat, hanging out and celebrating each other's success—but in a totally manly way, of course. They're terrific role models at a time when we're seeing an onslaught of loneliness and reports of a crisis of intimacy in male friendships. But still, there's a commercial, Hollywood cloud hanging over the celebrity bromances. We hear so few stories about noncelebrity male friends who offer a glimpse into their psyches.

For that reason, I am grateful to David and Yair for letting us traipse around in their lives. Their friendship proves that intimacy between two men is not only possible but affirming. It's a closeness we ascribe more often to our women friends. Which is to say, they're tight.

I love what Kate Leaver writes in her book, *The Friendship Cure:* "Men should have the right to intimate friendships if they want them, hang the traditional mores of masculinity."[24] She's so right. All of us deserve the right to cherish another human being, and that includes men and boys who love each other as friends.

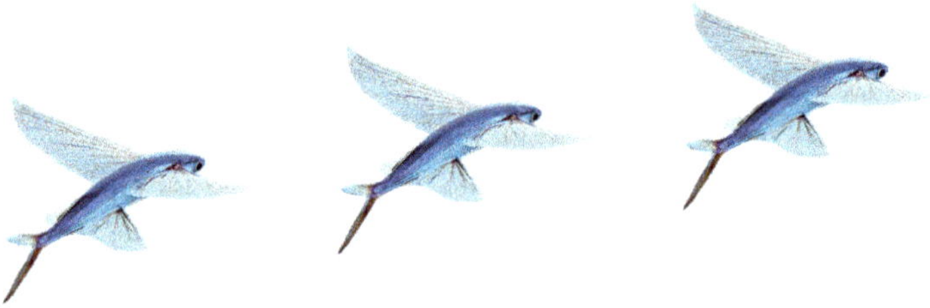

ACT III

15

Buck It

David and Yair kept a scribbled list of potential sales by the cash register. On super slow days, they'd pull out their notes, hoping this was the day "so-and-so would come back and buy such-and-such." Maybe the item was a pair of expensive sunglasses. They'd replay the customer's delight, the gushing, the solemn promise to return on a certain day. But more often than not, the gushers never came back. The sale never materialized. The product stubbornly sat on the shelf. The no-shows bummed them out, but what could two struggling retailers do?

They could always count on a return visit from Mandy, their first and most loyal customer. Every so often, she showed up with the next layaway payment clutched in her hand. She'd plunk down her money and beeline it to the rack with the new women's clothing. If she liked a dress, she'd finger the fabric and hold it up by the mirror. Then she'd hightail it to the skimboards or the sunglasses display. Whenever Mandy spotted something new, she lingered and gave the item her full attention. Sometimes she looked at the price tag and sighed.

The day she brought in her last payment, David made a show of folding her Rusty denim skirt, smoothing the creases. Yair placed the item, just so, inside a blue Bula bag and handed it to her. Once again there were fist bumps all around.

Mandy aside, David and Yair had a common-as-dirt problem. Foot traffic. There wasn't enough of it. Bula sat sequestered between other nondescript storefronts on the second floor of a vast, three-story mall. Customers had to know it was there and actively seek it out. A tight-knit community of locals knew and loved Bula, but there were only so many T-shirts and shorts they could buy. In marketing lingo, David and Yair needed to boost public awareness and build brand loyalty.

Any new business comes with a dismal survival rate.[25] More often than not, the success of a new business depends on its ability to get noticed—specifically, the ability to build buzz and engineer positive word of mouth. Other Aruban retailers in the same predicament bought ads in the newspapers, plastered their names on billboards, and blasted radio commercials. If they had an ounce of PR savvy, they might score an advertorial in one of the glossy tourist mags.

Retailers grazed like boring brown cows in the fields of traditional marketing rules: sell mainstream products, price as high as the market will bear, advertise, sell more stuff, repeat the formula. Almost every day, David and Yair got cold-called by reps eager to help them spend their advertising budget.

"Hey, want to do ads?" they'd ask.

"We don't do advertising." End of discussion.

A couple months before Bula's opening, David had skimmed a marketing book his dad left behind after a visit. The author beat the drum that mass-market advertising was corny and old school. The message stuck with David. From Day One, Bula adopted a no-advertising stance.

"Our policy gave the poor guys just trying to do their job an excuse to take back to their boss," David told me.

"Yeah, it was so efficient," Yair added. "They didn't have to do their spiel, and we didn't have to waste our time pretending to listen."

Purists to the core, David and Yair took another heretical stand: no sales or discounts, combined with everyday affordable pricing. Instead of artificially jacking up prices and then putting items on sale, a standard retailer practice, they opted for what I'd call *empathy pricing*. They lowballed Bula items so more locals could afford them. By not spending money on advertising and paying low rent for a mediocre mall location, David and Yair subsidized lower margins on their T-shirts and other house merchandise. If other retailers charged $4 for a sticker, they'd sell it for $2. At Bula, a $20 T-shirt sold for $14.

"We wanted as many people as possible to buy our house brand and get the Bula name out there," David explained.

Bula was all about the owners running their own show, staying unencumbered, and taking creative risks. I suspect it jazzed David and Yair every time they bucked a fad or sacred truth. If everyone else was turning right, they went left. They loved experimenting, playing with other people's ideas, hatching new ideas of their own. For several years, every time they sold a surfboard, bodyboard, or skimboard, they took a photo of the customer standing by the new purchase, all smiles. People loved seeing the picture of themselves or their friends festooned on the wall—Bula's own version of Mount Rushmore.

Whether the photo wall translated into more sales remained an open question. David and Yair didn't expect a tsunami of sales, not right away and maybe never. There was, in their minds, a good chance Bula would never break out from the noise, the clutter. But every day, David and Yair opened the shop with the same hypnotic tune playing in their heads: *Yes, the store's hard to find, but if we can get people coming here, we know we've got something.*

They put their faith in their early fans—one friend telling another friend, and on and on. One day, they hoped, Bula would start transmitting its own frequency through the static. Bula would *become* the signal.

"A Really Nice Place to Hang Out"

In good times and bad, David and Yair stubbornly refused to advertise. Instead of throwing money at typical boastful ads, they turned the equation upside down by supporting rising athletes. Sarah-Quita was the first local prodigy they sponsored. To defray the cost of traveling to her first off-island windsurfing competition, they handed her parents a check and gave her free T-shirts and other merchandise from the store. Sarah-Quita proudly put a Bula sticker on her sail and went on to win the event, the first in a long, unprecedented string of world windsurfing championships.

"Bula sponsored her because we liked her, not because it was trendy cool marketing," David told me. "She was happy to wear the T-shirt, and the visibility on the beach was good for us."

During one of my research visits to Aruba, David and Yair suggested I interview Sarah-Quita. She and I met up on opening day at the 2022 Hi-Winds event, an annual competition for windsurfers and kiters from around the world. I arrived a few minutes early at Fisherman's Huts, a rocky stretch of beach with timeworn huts at the water's edge. Windsurfers in the Hi-Winds event zipped across the relatively calm, flat waters typical of the lee side of the

Sarah-Quita Offringa is a twenty-two-time
(as of this printing) world windsurfing champion and
celebrated member of the Bula family.

island. The morning of our interview, the wind blew a constant twenty-three miles an hour out of the east, perfect conditions for the highly technical aerial stunts and acrobatics Sarah-Quita would perform later that day.

Sarah-Quita showed up for our interview in a lacy sleeveless top and blue twill shorts. Her zen calm struck me right away; she moved with the frictionless grace of a classically trained dancer. We sat in folding chairs under a spectator tent. It was difficult to hear each other over the beat of calypso music blasting from speakers, so we scooted our chairs closer to each other. Sarah-Quita opened right up about her memories of Bula.

Do you remember when you first went to Bula?

Not exactly. I was young, probably eleven or twelve. I tagged along with my brother. It was a really nice place to hang out…that's what I remember. I'd try on all the clothes, but I don't remember ever buying anything [laughter]. I just walked around with my big hair and tried to act all cool.

What did Bula do for you?

I got free Bula clothing, and then there was the day David and Yair handed my parents a check. The sponsorship was a handshake, that was all. Yair and David hooked me up with Billabong. They gave me boxes of clothing every so often. And I was happy to put Bula stickers on my sail. Today, I have a board sponsor, a sail sponsor . . . and many others. But, Bula was my very first sponsor. Anytime I went to the shop, they made me feel like I was part of the family. We're still all good friends.

Is there one distinct memory from the early days of your Bula sponsorship?

As a kid, I just thought the whole thing was really, really cool. It was big what they did for me back then. I remember one time I came back from winning a championship, and David was standing there at the airport, crying. He insists he didn't cry that hard, but I remember seeing the tears in his eyes [laughter].

Sarah-Quita makes it a habit to stock up on Bula gifts before leaving the island for a competition. Above, Bula's original three employees celebrate one of her 2009 wins. Dennis (in green) is fake crying in reference to David's famous tears after Sarah won her first championship.

Sponsorship gave Bula multiple, compounded advantages. First, as up-and-coming retailers, David and Yair didn't have to waste time and money on crass ads. The Bula name got carried along on a tide of local goodwill. Second, local sponsorships amplified a core value of the shop: authenticity. From the time David and Yair first swung their doors open to the public, they promised to serve the community. Giving money and swag to up-and-comers underscored Bula's commitment to lifting up the culture of the island.

David and Yair did the opposite of what most retailers do. They gave money to locals rather than grabbing for sales. That expression of authenticity proved contagious. By sticking to its core values, Bula became a brand magnet, attracting ever-widening circles of friends, family, and out-of-town acquaintances. All felt welcome, no matter how much money they had in their wallet. I believe Bula nailed long ago, and quite organically, the business model that today's brick-and-mortar shops still struggle to emulate: They elevated and humanized the retail experience.

16

Impact Zone

Early one morning, in late summer 2003, David and Yair jumped on their boards and paddled out into a wind-whipped sea. On the horizon, a container ship glided like an apparition toward Oranjestad. That day at Wariruri, the waves were bigger and more confused than usual—unpredictable, ragged, relentless—and sounded like thunderclaps exploding at close range. David and Yair paddled what felt like twenty minutes straight to make it through the impact zone, the term for the whitewater just shoreward of where the wave folds and breaks.

David and Yair got into a manic rhythm: paddle like hell, duck dive under the wave, fight back to the surface, grab a breath, and dive again. Even paddling like a windmill in a hurricane, it took all their strength to avoid getting pulled backward with every wave. When David and Yair finally found themselves "outside," beyond the impact zone, they saw four or five of their surfer buddies in the improbable calm of the lineup, laughing and shooting the breeze.

"Two or three of them were wearing shorts they had bought from a competitor," Yair told me. "Seeing those guys in their Quiksilver shorts crushed us. It was hilarious, really, how sensitive we were."

"Right, we had totally unrealistic expectations," David explained. "It wasn't enough that they bought boards with us, a low-profit item. We wanted them to spend every single dollar of their consumer income at Bula."

Neither managed to surf particularly well that morning in the challenging conditions. They took a pounding. Their arms felt rubbery, "noodled," when they got to shore. After the rush of getting worked over by the waves, they also felt a deep sense of calm when they climbed into Yair's rugged, sun-battered truck.

Lurching over the rutted, desert terrain toward Oranjestad, they talked honestly about Bula. The shop wasn't growing as fast as they'd hoped, barely breaking even. Just like their morning surf at Wariruri that day, they were paddling like crazy, but making no discernible headway. It struck them that they needed to figure out a way to pull Bula out of the churn. In the pressure of the moment, they came up with the idea for a slogan, something catchy but not gimmicky.

By the time they got to the shop, David and Yair had worked out the nuts and bolts of their new game plan. First, they'd design a cool and relevant wordmark and order a small inventory of T-shirts as their market test. If the shirts didn't sell, so be it. They'd just add it to their growing list of home-brewed flops.

"Wearing a Dushi Yiu! *Shirt Gave People a Sense of Pride"*

Yair: Printing *Dushi yiu!* on a T-shirt, well, that was a very strange thing to do. No retailer had ever done that. Papiamento was considered provincial and unsophisticated. If you wanted to be cool, you emulated American brands—the clothes, the fashions, what you saw on TV or the internet.

David: To an Aruban, *Dushi yiu!* is a fun little surfer-ish way of saying *Sweet!* or *Awesome!*

Yair: Right, right. *Dushi* is a multipurpose word. Arubans use *dushi* to praise a food, a nice person, or a festive occasion. The word is like a sweet friendly hug and part of the national identity of the island. Even its pronunciation sounds gentle and kind. The "d" is soft followed by a cooing vowel sound with no rise in pitch at the end.

David: Back in 2003, when I was learning to surf, locals would shout *Dushi yiu!* as a sign of respect when someone had a good ride. To my just-learning-Papiamento ears, the words sounded cool and kinda funny. The expression encapsulated all the reasons I loved being at the beach.

It's safe to say: If Bula's popularization of Dushi yiu! *hadn't gone viral and spread to the surrounding islands, the Curacaoan artist Francis Sling never would have painted this friendly mural. Photo credit: Sarah Harvey, journalist.*

Yair: I have to say this: David did an amazing job assimilating to Aruba. He learned Papiamento ridiculously fast and became perfectly fluent in no time, with a total command of the idioms and slang.

David: Most Arubans are multilingual, right? That made communication easier. I could get by speaking English and sprinkling in Spanish or random words from Papiamento.

Yair: Yeah, but a lot of expats get frustrated and revert to English. At one point, David went cold turkey and stopped speaking anything but Papiamento. At first the skaters and surfers replied in English to make communicating easier. But David didn't back down, and pretty soon, the surfers started correcting his Papiamento, encouraging him.

David: Hmm. I have no memory of doing that, but okay. I do remember everybody helping me. Gradually, I threw in more local phrases and less English.

Yair: David wasn't afraid of making mistakes or asking for help ... he had a beginner's mind. His ego wasn't so wrapped up in proving he could speak perfectly.

David: That's for sure [laughter].

Yair: Putting *Dushi yui!* on a shirt was an embrace of Aruban culture, an attempt to make Papiamento cool rather than turning away from it.

David: I wish I'd put more effort into the original T-shirt design. I slapped it together using a free font I found on the internet. We also underestimated how many shirts we needed to order. They sold out almost right away.

*Nikki, an early Bula employee, rocks a
classic* Dushi yiu! T, *circa 2010.*

Yair: Yeah, it blew us away. Arubans snapped up the shirt, and so did the other islands . . . Bonaire and Curaçao. Pretty soon the expression caught on with people moving to—or from—the Netherlands. Wearing the shirt gave people a sense of provenance. And it *really* got the Bula name out. People would come in just to buy that shirt.

David: To most tourists, *Dushi yiu!* was just gibberish. I guess that partially explains the appeal. It was different, a little mysterious.

Yair: Twenty years later, whenever we put *Dushi yiu!* on a new T or hat, it sells like crazy. I guess words can have charisma, just like a person, right?

Bula's breakthrough idea—adopting a Papiamento phrase as a brand identifier—got me thinking. Why do certain songs go viral? Certain companies become household names? And why do some social movements take root and spread, while others wither?

These questions fascinate Damon Centola, a University of Pennsylvania sociologist and author of *Change*, a book about social movements and entrepreneurial success.[26] To explain how ideas travel across communities, he describes information as a virus, infecting a few people in one neighborhood and spreading through social networks. If one influential person interacts with a lot of others, then that person acts as a super-spreader.

Centola cites the example of Oprah Winfrey sharing the news in April 2009 about an upstart social-media platform. Sitting next to Evan Williams, the cofounder of Twitter (now X), she said, "Can you believe all this tweedledee stuff going on? How did it come to life?" At the time, Twitter hadn't yet taken off, but by the end of the month, the platform counted twenty-nine million users. Oprah's celebrity endorsement set off a cascading series of fireworks explosions that spread rapidly through major communications networks.

Even a glancing contact can leapfrog the spread of information. Let's say you're at the airport, sitting next to someone who's waiting for the same flight. You're two strangers, but during the chance encounter, you learn about a great new app, podcast, or Netflix series and share it with that person next to you, who shares it with two friends, each of whom shares it with two more friends, and so on. It's just a casual conversation, but that's how a contact can trigger the widespread adoption of a product or service.

Centola's epidemiological model echoes Seth Godin's concept of the "sneezers," the key agents who spread social change. Sneezers are the influencers who tell all their colleagues, friends, or admirers about an innovation. In Bula's world, the hardcore surfers and skateboarders sneezed first. They went around the island proudly wearing the *Dushi yiu!* T-shirt. They looked cool. The shirts looked cool. Pretty soon, their families bought Ts, and when Bula came out with *Dushi yiu!* stickers, people put them on their boards, bicycles, and cars.

Overnight, it seemed, Bula was at the center of its very own fireworks explosion.

Ideas that spread, win. That's clear. But if ideas can spread like a virus, how is it that some don't leap from group to group? And conversely, why did the *Dushi yiu!* shirts explode into popularity—and stay popular for the next twenty years? For every viral success, there are millions of perfectly decent ideas and products that lie dormant. According to Godin, it's no accident some products catch fire and others don't. When an ideavirus spreads, it's often because all the pieces work together. Godin uses five filters to separate out the likely spreaders from the non-germinators:[27]

- How smooth and easy is it to spread the idea?
- How often will people "sneeze" it to friends?
- How tightly knit is the target group?
- Do they believe and support each other?
- How reputable are the people behind the idea?

All five of these elements worked in Bula's favor, especially the last one. David and Yair were young and charismatic. They loved surfing. The sport of surfing had an anarchist, sexy gestalt. People wanted to see them succeed— two likable entrepreneurs, working hard—so they hopped on the *Dushi yiu!* train. Which was easy, really. Putting down $10 for a T-shirt wasn't a big investment, and it was a simple philosophy to get behind. The expression radiated good vibes.

If the owner of a tacky souvenir shop had put *Dushi yiu!* on a dish towel, I seriously doubt the news would have gotten past the front door. Bula had all the viral ingredients such tourist traps typically lacked: authenticity, cool products, and a commitment to serving locals from all walks of life. In essence, David and Yair had already set the table for an ideavirus celebrating Aruba's street language.

Since 1986, when Aruba won its independence from the Netherlands Antilles and became a constituent country in the Kingdom of the Netherlands, citizens had grown increasingly fond of their native tongue. Papiamento evolved over hundreds of years as a language out of multiple influences: Arawak, British, Dutch, and Spanish with a sprinkling of Portuguese and African words. Using *Dushi yiu!* as a slogan, as simplistic as it may sound now, tapped into a deep national consciousness. The phrase ignited patriotic sentiments in the same way other countries revere their currency, official emblems, or flags.

Sarah-Quita proudly celebrates another windsurfing victory in her Dushi yiu! *shirt.*

David and Yair didn't just launch a $10 T-shirt. They gave birth to a Purple Cow idea. "Let's celebrate," they said. "Papiamento is cool. Surfing's cool. Let's be cool together."

So there you have it: a remarkable, easily adopted ideavirus. Just two simple words, printed on a shirt, turned the winds and the tides in a favorable direction for Bula's future.

17

Tipped

The expression "Nothing happens, then everything happens" alludes to the sensation we get when we slave away at something for the longest time. Then, in a split second it seems, all our hard work metamorphoses into tangible progress. That's what happened when David and Yair went to the movies in the fall of 2003. They had just bought their movie tickets when they noticed a group of teenage girls hanging out in the corner. One of them pointed their way and said, in a loud whisper, "Hey, look . . . the guys from Bula."

"I remember them giggling," Yair told me. "They were, like, fifteen or sixteen years old." Yair grew up on a small island with a population of about sixty-thousand people. It wasn't all that rare to get recognized. For David, the incident was totally unexpected and a bit shocking. He remembers thinking: *Maybe we're not so old we can't still be cool.*

"Yeah, it was kind of embarrassing," Yair added. "But definitely a good sign for the business that people knew us outside the tight circle of our friends."

"The tipping point is the magic moment when an idea, trend, or social behavior crosses a threshold, tips, and spreads like wildfire."[28]

MALCOLM GLADWELL, JOURNALIST, AUTHOR

I can easily imagine their delight when a gaggle of teenage girls went all gooey and starstruck in their presence. When it comes to coolness, it's all about external validation. You can't declare yourself cool. It's in the eye of the beholder—in this case, a cluster of giggling teenagers in a movie lobby. For two twenty-something friends minding their own business (literally and figuratively), what an affirming moment that must have been.

The duration of felt experience lasts a mere two or three seconds, about as long as it takes Paul McCartney to sing the words "Hey Jude." David and Yair's first "celebrity" sighting (they insisted I use quotes) transpired in a flash, but I dare say the event left an indelible effect. Independently, each insisted it wasn't such a big deal. I'm not convinced. Such soft-glow experiences often get crystallized into the memory bank. Like a cowlick, they stick with you. That's especially true, I think, of any memorable first—your first kiss, car, or romance.

For David and Yair, it must have felt magical when Bula started getting traction outside a small circle of their surfer buddies, skateboarders, and friends. They hadn't spent a cent on advertising or self-promotion. Grassroots support—which came from supporting locals, not pandering to wealthy tourists—was the viral ingredient that tipped the balance and launched them into their own private limelight.

18

Too Kind?

By early October 2003, just seven months after opening, David and Yair barely had time for a break. During the rare lulls in the action, they'd toss back a handful of nuts or grab a drink to keep the energy levels up. Then a new wave of customers would stampede into the shop. As introverts, they'd get depleted by the constant pressure of socializing all day long. But social exhaustion was a good problem for a retailer, they liked to say. Until it wasn't. One day Yair left for a doctor's appointment, leaving a stressed-out David marooned in the shop. The next morning they had an epiphany. Bula Surf Shop wouldn't survive as a two-man operation. They'd need to step out of their comfort zone—two best friends at the helm—and bring in outside help.

Many entrepreneurs make the mistake of trying to do everything themselves. They assume only they can handle the work. As the company grows, the escalating work can wear them down, physically and mentally. This is one of the hardest traps for even the most squared-away entrepreneur to detect, let alone avoid. There's an official name for start-up owners who turn into relentless solo operators or micromanagers. They're called "CEO monarchs," a term coined by Professor Jeffrey Sonnenfeld at the Yale School of Management.[29] For CEO monarchs, everything's about the founder's ego; their personal success is defined by the business. And it's all work and no play. Almost always, the business suffers, and so does their personal life.

David and Yair adopted the opposite philosophy. For them, work and play existed on a continuum. There were no hard lines separating the two. Of course, the Bula founders wanted to make money and run a thriving retail operation. But Bula Surf Shop was more about aspiring to an enjoyable lifestyle than proving themselves as business geniuses. So, once David and Yair realized they couldn't keep up with the work, they took the next indicated step of hiring their first employees.

Here, again, David and Yair didn't fit the mold. Finding and hiring good help is typically a nightmare for small-business owners—it takes time and effort with no guarantees. For David and Yair, recruitment was almost comically easy. Their talent pool came from Bula's original group of adolescent skateboarders. These were the kids who cut classes, cooled down in the AC, and watched surfing movies. A few of them had become fixtures at Bula. They'd faithfully show up at 10 in the morning and kill the whole day just for the chance of going surfing with David and Yair when the shop closed.

Bear in mind, this was before everyone had a smartphone (there was no TikTok to keep them occupied). To earn their keep, the teenagers volunteered to fold T-shirts or do tedious tasks like sorting stickers in the back room. Essentially, the merry band worked free, for months, to stay in David and Yair's good graces.

"So yeah, it wasn't hard for us to find nice people to work for us," David told me. "Our first employees practically forced themselves on us."

As idealistic new managers, with absolutely no clue about standard HR policies, David and Yair cobbled together an irregular set of employee guidelines:

Most-anything-goes dress code. If someone showed up for work in roller skates with a bikini top and skin-tight yoga pants, fine. But if an employee wore a faux surf brand like Hollister, a Midwestern offshoot of Abercrombie & Fitch, they got the stink eye. Wearing a lame brand violated Bula's authenticity code.

Higher-than-average wages. David and Yair overpaid their employees, most of whom had no retail experience or discernible life skills. They wanted to pay them well so they'd stay and maybe move up into a managerial role one day.

Subsidized meals. When David and Yair noticed employees ate sugary cereals for breakfast and a candy bar for lunch, they decided to offer them free meals. For years, they bought their employees a fortifying breakfast, lunch, and a midafternoon snack.

Surfing, mandatory. All employees were required to surf, period. They couldn't work at an authentic surf shop and not surf. The nonsurfers—the skaters, windsurfers, and skimboarders—learned on the job. David and Yair loaned them boards and took them surfing after work.

Bad moods and tantrums were tolerated, to a point. As long as they were friendly to customers and hid their bad moods from the public, employees didn't get in much trouble. David and Yair were willing to wait out the storm. As young bosses, they understood teenage angst—the raging hormones, emotional instability, and difficulties concentrating.

Wow. It sounds like a fun, amazing place to work, right? That was my first reaction. But then my skepticism kicked in. Sure, most companies function like families. From the outside, they may look similar and even formulaic. But on the inside, they're all uniquely complicated, with peculiar ways of doing things that can baffle outsiders. Bula's employee playbook struck me, someone who'd worked at traditional management consulting firms, as an epic example of generosity run wild.

Bula's ethos of friendliness reminded me of Yvon Chouinard's hands-off approach to running retailer Patagonia. He enforced no hard-and-fast rules other than getting the job done. At Patagonia, employees can stop working and go surfing when the surf's good. His critics question how he ever managed to build a multimillion-dollar business where the "inmates run the asylum." By Chouinard's own reckoning, Patagonia's employees are so independent, they are practically unemployable anywhere else.

I wondered if David and Yair ever worried they were being too permissive. Did employees ever take advantage of the friendly work environment? What advice would they give their younger selves? I wanted all the dirt.

"We Pampered the Hell Out of Them"

Yair: We hired for friendliness.

David: Our employees were part-timers. We knew they'd probably work a year or two for us and then go off to school. A few of them wanted to get on the university track in Holland. Most of them didn't have any ambitions other than making enough money to buy clothes and go surfing.

Yair: We made a conscious decision to pay an above-average living wage so that they'd want to stay.

David: We were incredibly generous. People can't believe we bought our employees meals. Over the years we shelled out tens of thousands of dollars on food.

Yair: At first, they were so grateful. But there was a diminishing return of gratitude.

David: They'd complain that they got chicken breasts for lunch again [laughter].

Yair: Yeah, we pampered the hell out of them.

David: We treated them almost like our children. We actually said: "You guys are family."

Yair: The problem was, the employer–employee relationship often got blurred. And that led to some issues. Like when they thought it was okay to come in late if they'd been out with a girlfriend. Can you imagine what it was like for these guys being in the prime of their nasty masculinity? They assumed we'd be happy for them that they'd gotten laid instead of pissed off that they showed up super late [laughter].

David: We had to learn the hard way that intense relationships with our employees were counterproductive.

Yair: We revised our thinking after we read a report that said the constant stress of functioning like a family can create a toxic work environment. One day we looked at each other and thought: *This is warped.*

*Left to right: Ashlin Ahlip, Ricardo "Cado" de Lannoy,
Yair, Dennis Schoneveld, and David.*

David: We decided to socialize less. In the beginning, we were in our
late twenties, and our employees were in their late teens, early
twenties. There wasn't a huge age gap. As we got older, new
cohorts of employees rotated in and the team stayed young.
Hanging out became less interesting for both sides. A cordial,
arms-length relationship made a lot more sense.

Yair: It's worth saying: Our first three employees worked for us for eight
years, and we are still very close to all of them to this day.

David: That's practically unheard of in retail. We got a lot better at
the simple routines, like I make a checklist every morning for
everyone. Employees seem to like the structure . . . you know,
checking off the boxes. I usually include a fun one like "enjoy
cake." We also give employees some freedom. Maybe they want
to design a display or pick the color for a new T-shirt. And they'll
tell us if they don't like a new shirt design . . . they're our target
demographic, so we use them like a focus group. We've tried other
things that didn't work, like threatening to dock someone's pay
if they showed up late or hung over. The standard punishments
didn't work at all. Friendly peer pressure has worked better . . .
teasing instead of harsh consequences.

A team-building excursion with Bula's
expanded crew, circa 2013.

Yair: We keep it fun, as much as that's possible, with a few non-negotiables: no stealing, bullying, or being mean to each other or customers. It's the same philosophy we started with: *We spend a third of our waking life at work. Why not spend that time with people we love?* Of course, most people don't have the luxury, but it's worth saying. Bula was born from that stated goal.

Can you be too nice? The question flashed to mind as I listened to David and Yair talk about their early days as managers. By their own admission, they sometimes went overboard pampering their first employees. They failed to set healthy boundaries . . . let unacceptable behaviors slide . . . struggled as disciplinarians. Certainly they suffered from the too-nice syndrome.

The dictionary defines *nice* as "pleasing, agreeable, delightful." Contrast this with the dictionary definition of *kind*: "having, showing, or proceeding from benevolence." Both words carry positive connotations, but the underlying motivations differ. Nice people, for example, hold the door open for others primarily out of a desire to create a favorable impression. Kind people do the same, but their motive extends beyond self-interest. They open a door because they see someone struggling. They want to spare the other person from extra effort or inconvenience. Their kind action comes from a place of benevolence.

Kindness unfairly gets a bad rap. People associate it with being weak or too soft. Daniel Lubetzky, the CEO of Kind Bar, makes a fascinating distinction between being nice and being kind: "The problem that exists in society is that people associate kindness with weakness," he said in a *Clear and Vivid* podcast with Alan Alda.[30] "And the reason that happens is *people confuse kindness with being nice*. You can be nice and be passive. But if you're kind, it requires an enormous amount of honesty. A nice person might . . . not tell you that there's something in your teeth or that you did something wrong. But the kind person will have the courage to tell you."

Lubetzky turned a $10,000 investment into a multibillion-dollar brand based on an unusual social mission to "be kind to your body, your taste buds, and to the world." His brand empire grew from two words you might find on a motivational plaque or poster: *Be Kind.*

> *"Kindness is* free *. . . and [yet]
> the return on the investment is bigger
> than any financial investment an
> entrepreneur can make."*[31]
>
> GUY RAZ, PODCASTER, AUTHOR, CREATOR

The kindness mantra echoes what Yair told me about wanting to work with people he loved. I don't mean to imply he and David were saintly every minute of every day. They had their fair share of screwups. But I dare to say that, from the start, both of them worked exceptionally hard to build kindness into Bula's DNA.

"A Kind of Religion"

*A portrait of twin brothers Karim and Maurice Neme,
organizers of Aruba's Electric Festival, for the cover of*
Xclusivo Aruba *magazine. Artist credit: Charis Tsevis.*

Maurice and Karim stationed themselves in front of the Royal Plaza Mall, sweating in the heat and plastering flyers on car windshields. Whenever people walked by, they'd shout out an invitation.

"Hey, come to a party!"

The brothers wanted a packed nightclub. Back in 2003, there were no such things as online tickets; they had to get them printed and collect cash. Maurice and Karim were young, with inexhaustible energy, but it was a crushing amount of work.

The twins spearheaded Aruba's party scene when electronic dance music and musical festivals were booming in the early 2000s. Maurice knew Yair from riding the bus to school. He called him Mr. Marine Science. If Maurice had a question about what was happening down underneath the water's surface, Yair loved sharing what he knew. Although Yair was a little older than Maurice, they were good buddies. So one day, just before an international music event, Maurice and his brother headed to Bula and pitched their idea.

Would Bula function as a pseudo-Ticketmaster for their big parties and musical events?

A partnership made a lot of sense, in theory. The twins were the cool guys doing parties, while Yair and David were the cool duo running an upstart surf shop. They'd use each other's marketing mojo for mutual benefit. For Bula, the logistics seemed simple enough: track tickets, hand out wristbands, and put cash into a box. Every so often, Maurice and his brother would swing by Bula and grab the money they needed to pay their expenses.

"They trusted us to handle thousands of dollars in cash," Yair told me. "It helped that I grew up on the island . . . people knew me and my family."

"It all started with Yair's friendship with the twins," added David. "There was that total trust."

David and Yair gave the Ticketmaster idea a try, hoping it might give Bula a shot in the arm early in 2003, before the business was fully established as an island fixture. Almost immediately, foot traffic picked up. From all parts of the island, people streamed into the shop. Before mega events, Bula attracted ticket lines out the door and around the corner, all day long. David and Yair hired dedicated workers to keep up with the volume of ticket sales.

But would ticket buyers browse and buy from the shop? That was an open question. Contrary to what I first thought, the majority of Bula's merchandise wasn't—and still isn't—worn while surfing. Arubans will tell you they love dressing up, looking good at family gatherings, holidays, any festive occasion. As soon as the *Dushi yiu!* shirts came out, the locals scooped them up in different colors. For a night out at a club, they'd match their green sneakers with their green *Dushi yiu!* T-shirt. The outfit was a fashion credential, but they didn't want to show up in the same outfit twice. So it was back to Bula for a new pair of jeans, a dressy halter top, or a collared shirt.

So yes. People didn't just buy tickets. As Maurice put it, "Going to Bula became a kind of religion" before a big event. He and his brother sold more tickets, a lot more efficiently, and Bula created a whole new culture of style on the island. Maurice described the relationship as a "match made in heaven."

Yair and David, too, were blown away by the response. "I guess people realized they could do cooler stuff in their life," reflected Yair. "How they dressed for the concerts—their pride in their appearance—was all part of that."

"Selling tickets at Bula was an early grassroots idea that really paid off for us," David added. "We were just starting out, and we needed all the foot traffic we could get. Our association with the cool guys doing the high-budget events made us seem cooler. It was a total win all around."

19

Mutterings, Meals, and Mentors

One gusty morning, late in 2003, the GONE SURFING sign stayed up longer than usual.

David and Yair normally got to the shop in plenty of time to open at 9:30 a.m. sharp. But on this day, they took a detour to their accountant's office for Bula's first annual financial review. Their tax accountant, a glorified bookkeeper, kept them waiting on stiff-backed chairs flanking a desk piled high with papers.

She muttered under her breath as she pored over Bula's 2003 sales figures. David and Yair watched her fingers fly up and down the keys of the adding machine with robotic precision. Her nondescript office had low ceilings, no windows, and a rackety air-conditioner cranked high. David and Yair tried not to fidget.

"Sitting there was almost as bad as waiting at the dentist's," David told me. "We wanted to get back to the shop . . . the fun stuff." He gave Yair a puzzled look when the accountant whispered, "*Lucrativo.*" She mumbled the word again as she punched more numbers into the adding machine.

"We didn't have a yardstick for, like, whether Bula was working as a business," Yair recalled. "We were too deep in the trenches, running things."

When the accountant finished her calculations, she glanced up at David and Yair over her maroon eyeglasses. They braced themselves for her verdict. She gathered up the stack of pages, tapped them into shape, and slid them into a folder. Then she dropped the bomb.

"Well, Bula's *hopi lucrativo* ["very profitable"]."

David and Yair locked eyes. Score!

"If I'd known, we'd have done something different with your tax setup." Her tone sounded vaguely judgmental. As it turned out, the shop would have been much more *lucrativo* if she had done a half-way decent job handling Bula's taxes. But David and Yair didn't know that then.

She stood up and showed them out, all smiles. "*Pabien,*" she said, shaking their hands. David and Yair cracked jokes all the way back to the shop, dropping *lucrativo* nonsensically into their conversation.

Hey, look at that graffiti on the side of that building. Lucrativo!

Lucrativo became an instant inside joke, a Bula staple. "Yeah, we loved the sound of the word," Yair reflected. "But it wasn't like we were gonna become billionaires running a surf shop."

I gathered they felt a mixture of tremendous relief and guarded optimism that morning.

"*Lucrative* is a relative term, of course," David told me. "But yeah, it was super encouraging to hear Bula might actually make it as a business."

To celebrate the New Year, and Bula's first year in business, Yair's father invited David and Yair for a fancy meal at his favorite restaurant, Chalet Suisse. The main dining room was the height of old-style European comfort and warmth, with padded booths, white tablecloths, and a friendly wait staff who knew Adolf by name. Since the restaurant opened in 1989 as a recreation of a Swiss chalet, he'd sampled nearly every one of the restaurant's signature dishes. Rack of lamb. Chicken cordon bleu. Traditionally prepared schnitzel. Beef stroganoff. Stuffed grouper medallions, caught fresh that day in local waters.

Yair's father had recently been diagnosed with Parkinson's disease, but on that festive occasion at Chalet Suisse, he was in robust good cheer.

"Get whatever you want," he said, gesturing toward the menu.

Debbie and Ana weren't keen on beef or meat in general, so the Bula guys most likely ordered steaks as a rare treat. As a notoriously enthusiastic eater, Yair probably finished with a gooey dessert like the chocolate mousse or the crème brûlée. Although he claimed to prefer savory dishes, Yair would scoop up every last morsel of any sweet confection. David liked to rib him for his habit of leaving crosshatches of spoon marks on the bottom of his dessert plate.

"He'd run his spoon over the custard, back and forth, methodically, like a lawnmower," David told me. "He didn't want to miss a thing."

Yair's father surprised them when, over coffee and dessert, he broached the topic of how quickly Bula had established itself. "He normally wasn't an effusive person," Yair told me. "It was rare for him to express such positive approval."

Adolf assured them they were doing great, Bula was doing great. Yair remembered pushing back. He tried to downplay Bula's success.

"We're happy," he told his father. "But we're not going to get rich . . ."

His father cut him off. "Oh no, this is exactly how you get rich."

Adolf left them with a prediction: Bula was doing so well, they should expect a wave of copycats. His advice: *Never, ever take your foot off the pedal.*

Yair's father was a fascinating man. Adolf had built a nearly legendary reputation as a first-generation Aruban who built a local empire out of thin air. He had a knack for sensing the potential in neglected parcels of land, in buildings in a state of charmless decline, and even in the downtrodden people he met along the way.

Among his many other interests, Adolf had learned martial arts in the States and established the first karate school in Aruba. The gym took young kids from beginner to black belt. Many of them practically grew up in that school and, later, enrolled their own kids there. Over the years, the karate dojo instilled confidence and skills in Arubans from every conceivable background and nationality. Adolf had seen countless people and companies rise to success only to get thrashed by complacency or smarter competitors.

"This success thing, it's easy come, easy go," he told them as he picked up the check.

I suspect that, like most entrepreneurs, David and Yair already had an inborn mistrust of Bula's early success. I'd describe them as hopeful realists with a deep cautious streak. Bula was still an upstart business, only a year or so old. They had made a risky leap off the cliff of entrepreneurship. The Bula prototype was built with its engines firing. The business had taken off faster than they ever imagined, but they didn't know why. There was no replicable formula. They were just doing what made sense in the moment.

"We worried it would all evaporate," Yair confessed.

They were in a crucible period as cofounders. A gauntlet of tests and traps, twists and turns, awaited them. Yair's father warned them to stay resilient, and maybe a little scared, so they'd spring back to fight another day.

On a whim, David did a quick Google search of typical retail sales on a square-foot basis. It was late January 2005. Bula had lost all vestiges of its under-nourished look. They'd packed every inch of the small space with merchandise. Yair's hanging racks were stuffed full of boardshorts, Ts, and sun-protective rash guards in a rainbow of colors. A flotilla of surfboards hung from the ceiling in neat rows. By the entrance, the Reef sandals practically flew off the shelves. All day long the cash register rang up sales at a steady clip.

David was shocked when he applied the industry sale-per-square-foot formula to Bula.

"Yair, you're not going to believe this." David motioned him over to his laptop. "Look at this!"

The shop was making $1,000 a square foot, the equivalent, at the time, of a high-end jewelry store. They looked at each other in amazement, then got back to work.

Later that same day, they booked a reservation for four at Amazonia, a Brazilian steak house. During Bula's first few months, Ana and Debbie had seen little of their handsome boyfriends. David and Yair had devoted nearly every ounce of their waking energy to the start-up.

"They'd been incredibly understanding," Yair told me. "It was time, maybe past time, to thank them."

For the couples' celebratory dinner, David and Yair chose a carnivore lover's paradise with a well-provisioned salad bar for vegetarians. Amazonia had high ceilings, rustic beams, and giant pots of palm trees circling the dining room. At night, lamps cast a flattering circle of light on dining tables the color of fudge. Each table had its own wooden pepper mill painted green on one end, red on the other. Waiters magically appeared with endless rounds of sizzling meat platters until the diners put up the red stop signal.

Ana remembered laughing when Yair suggested Amazonia.

"He was, and still is, a big meat lover," she told me. "He liked going there because I normally don't cook meat at home." Ana felt sorry for the waiter-in-training tasked with proffering a tray of grilled pineapple slices. "Everyone kept saying 'no thanks' except me," she recalled. "I said, 'Sure, give me double.'"

Neither Ana nor Debbie remembers much else about that first dinner, except that it grew into a pleasing ritual. Every few months, the four of them got together to celebrate another Bula milestone. Much to their amazement, the shop kept breaking its own records, punching well above its weight class.

"David and Yair never discussed how Bula was doing, not directly," Ana explained. "They'd just say, 'Let's all go out for a nice dinner.' It was never about the money." I gathered they all considered the subject of money-making tacky. Why bring it up and ruin a nice meal?

The date nights weren't an extravagant gesture, but they showed David and Yair hadn't forgotten their promise to make Bula a friendship-first proposition. Emily Langan, a Wheaton College professor of communications, argues that we need our good-vibe rituals, no matter how ordinary. When it comes to friendship, we are often ritual deficient, bereft of the rites that force families together over Thanksgiving, Christmas Eve, or summer reunions at the lake house. We're not in the habit of elevating the practices of friendship, she asserts. Yet she's fascinated by how even simple interactions—weekly coffee meetups, monthly hikes, regular dinners—can bond people in unexpected and profound ways. Langan makes the point that friendship rituals "should be similar to what we do for other relationships."[32]

I wonder how differently things might have gone if David and Yair had put their significant others on autopilot during Bula's hectic start-up phase. It would have been easy to let socializing slide to the bottom of their priority list, and then what? Asymmetries of time and attention can continue only so long without doing harm to a relationship. And if Ana and Debbie had felt excluded or ignored, then the whole Bula experiment might have veered off course.

The steak dinners looped Ana and Debbie into Bula's burgeoning success. Over time, the simple act of sharing a meal brought Ana and Debbie closer. Trust grew. They confided in each other, supported each other emotionally.

"We Slowly Learned to Be Both Less Stubborn and Less Idealistic"

Yair: It was incredibly lucky for us that a major competitor went out of business not long after we opened. Beach Bum was the exclusive Billabong dealer on the island. When the owner closed the shop, we saw the opportunity to pick up the brand. Billabong was head and shoulders above every other surfwear company in the industry.

David: The Billabong rep, Tony, lived in Puerto Rico. Yair wrote him a heartfelt email, introducing us. It wasn't the typical business approach of bragging about annual sales and ending with something confident like, "We'd like to add Billabong to the mix." Bula was so small, a blip on a manufacturer's spreadsheet. We had zero bragging rights.

Yair: Right! I took a ridiculously sentimental approach: two pages about Bula as the hub for the surfing community. I included personal stuff about both of us and our passion for surfing. Tony was kinda touched by the sincerity, I guess.

David: Tony was one of the last straight shooters in the surfing industry. He refused to sell to us until Beach Bum officially closed. Then he went out on a limb and gave us a shot.

Yair: Signing with Billabong was a real eye-opener. Before having a top-tier surf brand, to make any sale took a lot of coaxing: *Those boardshorts fit you great.* Or: *That's a beautiful red.* But anything with the Billabong logo sold without much effort.

David: We drove Tony nuts when we put in ridiculously small orders. "You guys are doing the picket fence," he'd say, complaining how we would blindly just order one or two of each size. We selected a few of most everything because we were such a small market. Most Bula regulars are part of the same social circle, and our theory was that they don't want to show up at the beach wearing the same pair of trunks as six other guys. Tony pounded it into us: *Put in bigger orders. They'll sell.* It was a revelation to us when wealthy European tourists started coming to Bula. We had a myopic view that only surfers and skaters would want to shop here.

Yair: Billabong was booming, at its apex from 2004 to about 2011. But we didn't know how to order. We were mistakenly super focused on price. We had the mindset of impoverished college kids. Forty dollars for a pair of shorts was the most we thought people would pay. So we studied the catalog and ordered the basic black or red shorts. It took a few experimental orders to realize people really wanted the $55 model with the wild designs.

David: Tony convinced us that people would come to Bula because it was cool, not necessarily cheap. . . . If customers wanted something cheap, they could go down the street.

Yair: Tony was, and is, an absolute legend in our minds. But we, stubbornly, didn't always listen to him. He'd call us on the phone and gently say: "Don't blow it!" Tony was our doorway to learning how to stock, how to price, even how to put out the T-shirts on tables so the designs showed. Getting access to Billabong, through Tony, was our first step toward becoming a professionally run surf shop.

David: We slowly learned to be both less stubborn and less idealistic, in roughly equal measure. And this evolution made us less frustrated and more profitable.

(20)

Point of No Return

"Where's Astor?" David asked, as he scooped up an armful of shirts still on hangers and headed out the door.

In Aruba, shops close on Sunday. The Royal Plaza Mall was deserted except for the beehive of activity at Bula. This particular Sunday called for an all-hands-on-deck rallying of the troops: empty out the shop, stuffed to the rafters with merchandise, and transport Bula to its new expanded location right next door. The former tenant, a souvenir shop, had tanked during the 2008–2009 global recession. Untold numbers of retailers had gone bankrupt at the Royal Plaza and elsewhere on the island.

David and Yair took the leap into the empty space with hardly a backward look. It was one of their signature counterintuitive moves. They weren't aiming for global domination, just a little more breathing room. Now they'd have a new takeoff spot, double the size. Plus, they were sick of living in the shadows of their nemesis, a bigger, glitzier surfwear shop on Main Street. Every time a customer walked into Bula with a shopping bag from Panache, it curdled their spirits.

"Panache's owners had the upper hand because they started before us and stocked a wider variety of brands," Yair told me. Panache was the annoying competitor Yair's father had warned them about over dinner at Chalet Suisse.

"They were always trying to copy our strategies and steal our brands and customers," David told me.

With more space, Bula stood a better chance of duking it out with its archrival. In the weeks leading up to the move, David and Yair plotted out Bula's new floor plan on graph paper. With growing excitement, they scientifically calculated the traffic flow around the displays. The aisles had to be just wide enough for stress-free browsing. And, of course, they needed to find the perfect spots for Yair's driftwood racks.

Ash, Cado, and Dennis staggered in to help with the big move after a night of heavy partying. They were red-eyed but game. Only one, Bula's youngest new hire, failed to show up on time.

"My mom told me I had to give the dog a bath," he'd told Yair when he sauntered in, two hours late. Astor was a chill, blond Adonis with heart-melting green eyes. High school girls would stop by Bula just to flirt with him.

Yair told me he'll never forget Astor's excuse for his late arrival the day of the big move. Apparently, Mr. Green Eyes (his official Bula nickname) hadn't bathed the dog in a month. What was a guy to do?

"Astor apologized but I could tell he didn't mean it," Yair remarked. "I gave him a hard time about his tardiness, but he had such a big, likable personality . . . it was impossible to stay mad at him for long."

*Astor (foreground) and Dennis enjoy a rare moment
of quiet at Bula's new location in 2009.*

Astor's wash-the-dog explanation would become a Bula cult classic, topping all other creative excuses. From that day forward, David and Yair amused themselves by keeping a hit list of most popular reasons for tardiness or no-shows. Most of Bula's workers came from a small pool of well-meaning underachievers, aged seventeen to twenty, with no serious academic ambitions. Many had never before worked a real job. They didn't have a grip on what was acceptable or unacceptable, even something as basic as showing up for work. New Bula employees invariably presented their excuses as a self-evident truth, on par with the gravity of a car accident or life-threatening illness.

> *I forgot to check the schedule.*
> *My cell phone battery died.*
> *My alarm didn't go off.*
> *I couldn't find my charger.*
> *I have a bad hangover.*
> *I have cramps.*

As an avid supporter of women's rights, David rolled with the menstrual excuse until Debbie got wind of his benevolence. Her perspective: They've got to power through the pain.

"She taught me to be less of a feminist," David said, laughing.

He told me he learned to lean on Yair to help smooth over the daily rough patches with employees. "Yair's the diplomat," he explained. "He can mold employees into the Bula way of doing things, while I'd sometimes expect too much, too soon."

Astor wasn't the only Adonis at Bula. After some heavy prodding from
Cado, Dennis struck up a conversation with Rachel Brathen while she
was browsing one day at Bula in 2011. The sparks flew in both directions.
Rachel and Dennis now live in Sweden with their two children.
Dennis draws from his business experience at Bula to help run
Yoga Girl, Rachel's sensationally popular lifestyle brand.

"I Don't Think I've Ever Been So Stressed by Anything"

Yair: During the 2008–2009 recession, when we moved next door, we were pretty freaked out by Panache. We were flying the Billabong flag, and they had Quiksilver. It was a head-to-head combat between the two absolute giants of the surf industry. They had Roxy, Quiksilver's super-popular women's brand. Women's clothing has always been a pretty crappy category for us.

David: Panache was trying to copycat us, just like your dad predicted. They wanted to appeal to core surfers. But they didn't sell any boards or know anything about surfing. They pushed the lucrative mass-marketed labels . . . you know, the boardshorts you could get on sale at Macy's or JC Penney. We would get very peevish and angry about that. We were just insecure.

Yair: Right, we viewed Panache as the most formidable opponent. In retrospect, it was like when people thought the Russians were invincible during the Cold War, but then they just kind of fizzled out.

David: Our sales reps kept telling us, "You're kicking ass. Don't worry so much." But what we were really worried about had much more to do with our immigration problems.

Yair: Right, now that was a true crisis. It's hard to get a permit to live in Aruba. There's always been an influx of immigration, and more than enough local people seeking jobs. In the early 2000s, the party in power came up with a strict, anti-immigration rule. As an expat, you could only live three years in Aruba without the right permit.

David: I could stay because I had an investor permit as a business owner. But Debbie only had a temporary permit. When her grandmother got sick, she couldn't fly to the States because her permit had run out. The authorities told her she could leave, but prohibited her to return to the island. I was sick about that. I don't think I've ever been so stressed by anything. We had to keep going back to court, pushing a boulder up the hill.

Yair: That was a mega stressful period for all of us. Ana faced the same threat of imminent deportation that Debbie did.

David: We'd invested so much into Bula at that point. And the shop was going gangbusters.

Yair: We ended up solving it by getting married about the same time the government adopted a more favorable policy on immigration.

David: At that point we had a paper trail, a legal history. We were pretty confident the immigration issue would get resolved by the time we moved into the new location.

Yair: It was a happy coincidence there was a change in political power.

David: Yeah. We were well beyond the point where either of us could resume our old lives. Those lives were gone. We'd crossed the Rubicon.

At the time of the immigration crisis, Bula's sales were growing at a clip of 25 percent a year. The shop had established deep, well-nourished roots in the community. Now on the brink of even greater financial success, David and Yair faced the threat of deportation. In one of my usual morning WhatsApp texts, I asked Yair if he'd ever considered running Bula solo if immigration issues had forced David and Debbie to leave Aruba. As an Aruban native, he was the logical choice to keep Bula humming right along, right?

Well, no.

Yair left me an unusually long voice message, during which he compared Bula to a table with four legs. "If you saw off one leg, the whole thing topples," he said, apologizing that he couldn't come up with a better metaphor. The whole point of Bula, he insisted, was to do something fun with a best friend. "We weren't interested in just running a retail operation." The immigration uncertainties hit them right in the gut, he told me, "because we didn't know what the hell we would do with our lives if Bula failed."

I love how Yair defined failure. It didn't matter that Bula was succeeding spectacularly as a business. What mattered was preserving the friendship, followed by doing something good for the community and having fun. Financial gain wasn't the end game, nor was individual success. Bula was built on an odd premise: *mutual reliance*. As a couple of rebels, joined in an outlandish quest, they knew they'd never make it on the strength of their individual talents alone. They needed the X factor of their friendship—and the entire Bula community—to thrive.

Making this surfboard, the first of many, helped
Yair recover from a depressive episode.

At the time of Bula's immigration troubles, Yair spiraled into another severe bout of depression. He could barely drag himself to the shop each day.

"I felt doubly bad because David had to pick up all the slack," he told me. One day a new customer wandered into the shop and spent a long time looking at the surfboards. He happened to mention he'd just made a wooden surfboard from a kit he got from Grain Surfboards in Maine. That piqued Yair's curiosity. The day before, Yair's psychologist had suggested he might try using his hands, building something, as a way out of the depression.

"Shit, that's exactly what I need to do," Yair said to himself. When his surfboard kit arrived, he got hooked. "I loved the smell of the wood and using the tools."

It took him just a few months to build the board *(see photo)*, which he gave to David for his birthday. By then, Yair's depression had lifted. He gained a huge sense of accomplishment out of the project.

"That board kicked off my whole woodworking obsession," he reflected. "It was such a weird coincidence that I got the idea from a random customer in the shop."

Mutual reliance + *lucky breaks* + *arbitrary advantages* isn't a success formula we hear much about, unless you're a Malcolm Gladwell fan. In his bestselling book, *Outliers: The Story of Success*, Gladwell debunks the myth of individual merit as the chief predictor of success.[33] He uses the metaphor of a forest to illustrate his point. The tallest trees don't become the tallest because they're just naturally better than every other tree, he argues. A good start—a hearty acorn—isn't enough for saplings to grow big and strong. They grow to great heights because of their environments—healthy soil, water, and sunlight. Luck plays a role, too. The tallest trees don't fall prey to hazards like insects, lumberjacks, or natural disasters. Like humans, the tallest trees rise up because of a favorable environment and an intricate web of support systems.

As a culture, we celebrate prodigies and lone geniuses. Rugged individualism is quintessentially stars-and-stripes American. We're encouraged to put our self-interest before any other obligations: *I need to put on my oxygen mask before I can put on yours.*

Esther Perel, the Belgian psychotherapist and *New York Times* bestselling author, asserts that many of us are raised for autonomy. Consciously or not, we absorb the message we've got to rely on ourselves. In the end, it's all about self-determination. The *autonomy mindset* tells us we are alone in the world. And this influences the way we organize our relationships, our concept of give and take, and the extent to which we rely on others.

By contrast, the *loyalty mindset* stems from the belief we are never truly alone. We can lean on others in times of distress. "The loyalty [premise]. . . tells us we owe a lot of things to a lot of people," Perel says. "When we have a problem, we don't think, 'What can I do?' Instead we ask, 'Who can help me get through this?'"[34]

The autonomy versus loyalty mentality intrigues me, and not just because of the implications for David and Yair. It dredges up a memory of a troubling incident with my best friend, Abby, from high school. Our complicated and fragile friendship started unraveling after I weaseled out of an invitation to join her and another friend of hers in an after-school study group. Abby was hoping for a little help from her friends, fellow sufferers in a precalc class. Our teacher was a stern taskmaster and didn't believe in makeup tests.

In hindsight, I realize Abby was operating from an "others can help me" mindset. By contrast, I was in pure survival mode, terrified of getting a bad grade in that class. I wasn't willing to forfeit my private study time for a communal groping in the dark. What good could come of three math phobics huddling over their homework at the kitchen table? I'm not proud to admit this, but protecting my grade point average mattered more than showing up for Abby. What never occurred to me: *I'll do this [dumb thing] even though it inconveniences me, because you're important to me.*

An unspoken friction grew between us. Abby dropped me as a best friend. I got replaced by the friend who'd said yes to her homework club. The two of them are still best friends. And to this day, I still feel queasy about how she and I just drifted apart, leaving a wormy mess of unresolved issues behind us. The point of my story is this: Unlike marriage or parenthood, the terms of friendship are open-ended and entirely voluntary. We choose to be friends, and we choose to show up for each other . . . or not. In a culture that's so individualistic, friendships can default to a path of least resistance. And it's tricky just getting on the same wavelength about what we can reasonably expect from each other.

*"The values of the world we inhabit
and the people we surround ourselves with
have a profound effect on who we are."* [35]

MALCOLM GLADWELL, JOURNALIST, AUTHOR

David and Yair sidestepped these common minefields by making friendship a priority in work and in play. Even when they didn't feel like it, they reliably showed up for each other . . . lifted each other up . . . filled in each other's blanks. The notion of self-made never seemed to cross their minds, and a loyalty mindset came quite naturally. So when immigration policies threatened Bula's survival, and their futures, they knew just what to do. They hitched their life rafts together, tightened the straps, and rode out the turbulence.

Fending Off the
Energy Vampires

Your friendly little Aruban surf shop. It's a winning brand statement for an underdog surf shop that had chugged its way through a global recession. In Bula's new expanded space, there was more of everything to contend with: more stuff, more staff, and more customers streaming through the shop. But even at twice its size, Bula was still tiny.

Day after day, David and Yair worked hard to deliver on their promise: *We may be small, but we're friendly, plus we sell lots of cool merchandise.* Bula's signal had to be powerful and consistent, because that's what any strong brand does to stay competitive.

Other Aruban retailers typically sanded down the rough edges of their products and services to appeal to the broadest possible audience. They filled the slot of safe and boring, the vanilla ice cream of retail, while Bula served up a creamy concoction of spice, nuts, and caramel sweetness.

But it wasn't all sweetness and light running a surf shop. On certain cruise ship days, for example, Bula got hit by an invasion of tourists milling around, browsing. The shop would look jammed, but no one bought anything. These conditions David and Yair deemed "smoky"—lots of smoke, but no fire.

Typical cruise ship tourists, especially those on a budget, were oblivious to Bula's charms. The Purple Cow signal was lost on them.

"They tended to move in droves, from shop to shop," Yair told me. "If they didn't see a T-shirt with an iguana riding a jet ski while drinking a beer, they left."

On smoke-filled days, David and Yair had to work extra hard to keep the vibe friendly. It wasn't easy to stay true to their philosophy of being welcoming. As a defense against smoke inhalation, they sometimes reverted to the adolescent humor that bonded them in their early college days. They'd text each other images of a smokestack, a burning house, or the daily specials at Smokey Joe's, a local restaurant.

"It wasn't a super intellectual thing," David laughingly admitted.

Water was another private signal of theirs, inspired by one of their favorite writers, David Foster Wallace. They loved his bullshit-free 2005 commencement speech at Kenyon College, "This Is Water," in which he makes the case for living a compassionate, authentic life. His brief talk starts with the story of two young fish merrily swimming along. They happen to meet an older fish headed the other way, who nods and says, "Morning boys, How's the water?" The two young fish keep swimming and, after a time, one of them looks over at the other and says, "What the hell is water?"

David and Yair don't remember how it started, but one day they adopted the phrase, "This is *our* water." On peak stress days, they'd send each other GIFs. Kevin Costner in *Waterworld*. The movie poster of *Jaws*. A picture of a motorboat nose down in a muddy river.

"Any image about water made the point," Yair told me. "Yeah, this was our reality. These were the waters we were swimming in."

"It was our simplistic way of fending off the energy vampires of the day," David added. Vampires came into the shop in many shapes and forms. Hagglers, for example. They'd storm through the door, on a kamikaze mission to score a bargain. David remembered one customer in particular. He came in carrying an overstuffed shopping bag in each hand.

"I'll give you one dollar for that sticker," the man said. David told me the haggler kept jabbing his finger at the glass sticker case, calling attention to the expensive dive watch on his wrist.

"We don't discount," David said, polite but firm. His face flushed bright pink. Even the newest employee knew what that meant: trouble.

"I don't pay retail," the customer said, raising his voice.

"Sorry about that," David replied. "That's what it costs, three dollars." David's face turned a deeper shade of red. For a few tense seconds, they stood their positions. Neither flinched. The haggler opened his mouth to say something, but then caught himself. Angrily, he scooped up his shopping bags and huffed out of the store.

The absurdity of the incident delighted David and Yair, and employees, too. The haggler became Bula's legendary "I don't pay retail" guy. Another notorious customer, a local, insisted on exchanging his worn flip-flops for a new pair. Expecting resistance, he launched into an elaborate explanation of how, back in the day, Arubans would exchange three fish for a goat.

"We didn't know what he was talking about," Yair recalled. "But we gave him a new pair. That was the Bula way."

Then there was the rich Dutch tourist who burst out of the dressing room in a pair of Billabong boardshorts.

"Look at this," he muttered, looking down at the shorts. A couple of employees came over and peered at his torso. The boardshorts looked like they fit him perfectly.

"*Zie je? Dit probleem,*" he muttered in exasperation, pointing to the waistband. *You see? This problem.* To him the issue of the ill-fitting shorts was self-evident and obvious for all to see. He demanded to try on a different size. An employee brought him a few more shorts to try on.

A short time later, he stormed out of the dressing room again with fresh complaints about the fit of the waistband. After trying on a few more styles and sizes, he gave up and slipped on a pair of leather sandals. He complained about the separation between the toes. Another pair made his foot go forward too far. There was always a problem. He left the store empty-handed and in a sour mood. That day he gained lasting notoriety as Bula's "Dit Probleem" customer.

"Some people will never find satisfaction in a surf shop, or anywhere else for that matter," Yair told me in a philosophical moment. His comment struck at a core tenet of living well: Don't let the malcontents make you feel small. You can't fix them, so try to see the humor and move on.

I just love Yair's philosophy, a classic Stoic mindset. If we accept that bad stuff will happen, out of our control, we'll never be disappointed. Setting reasonable expectations allows us to maintain a healthy sense of balance and perspective. This philosophy guided Yair and David when they refused to join the stampede to the fancy new malls.

"People Thought We Were Nuts for Not Joining the Gold Rush."

David: Some people wondered why we didn't just open up a second shop when the big malls opened up in the hotel area. Before 2011, the major retail was on Main Street in downtown Oranjestad. When developers built the malls in Palm Beach, a lot of retailers jumped on board. They saw it as a cash grab, easy money. Why not? People told us: "Of course, you'll go there, get all this tourist traffic, and make lots more."

Yair: Yeah, no regrets. But people definitely thought we were nuts for not joining the gold rush. Panache did, but we weren't freaked out by that. They effectively handed us the torch. Now the owners couldn't be fully in either location.

David: We saw expansion as a dilution of our secret sauce. You know, we represented surfing, and that required us to show up every day. We wanted to keep giving really good customer service. To open a second store and repeat what we were doing, well, that never really crossed our minds in any serious way. Ditto the idea of franchising or opening up shops in Holland and Curaçao. We hung onto the mystical idea of running a true surf shop. Small, one location, both of us running it.

Yair: Adding locations would have made our roles totally different, you know? It would have made us more like executives, rather than two guys running a mom-and-pop business, having fun. I'm really glad we didn't expand. We would have created so much extra stress for ourselves.

When David and Yair refused to join the gold rush, they defied a sacred tenet of business: Big equals great. Most companies are determined to grow fast, expand geographically, and get as big as possible, as fast as possible. As humans, our brain chemistry is wired for acquisition. When we engage in addition, also called acquisitiveness, we stimulate a reward center in the brain—it's like a drug that activates a reward pathway. This happens whether we're growing a business, buying something on Amazon, or eating a rich dessert. Our brain tells us: *Yes, add more stuff, it's going to feel great.*[36]

Reflecting back on his fifty years building Patagonia, CEO and founder Yvon Chouinard admits the "hardest thing in the world is to simplify your life because everything pulls you to be more complex."[37] Despite his own best efforts to stay small, his clothing company grew too fast and hit a wall during the recession of the 1980s. Patagonia ran out of money. Yvon feared his business would fail. Of course, we all know Yvon went on to transform Patagonia into a global mega brand, but his point stands. Whether we're planning a vacation, making a club sandwich, or creating a strategic plan, simplification doesn't come easily to us, while addition is psychologically pleasurable.[38]

David and Yair did something counterintuitively brilliant when they marketed Bula as Aruba's friendly *little* surf shop. Instead of hiding Bula's smallness, like a shameful defect, they morphed it into a differentiator. Unlike mass-merchandise shops, Bula established itself as a refuge where people could browse without feeling overwhelmed by choices or pressured in any way. David and Yair's minimalist business strategy reminds me of the art of the bonsai. From Bula's earliest days, they seem to have developed the habit of trimming back their priority list, pruning strategically to focus on healthy growth.

They somehow managed to avoid the usual time sucks: proliferating to-do lists, getting distracted from every direction, and mindlessly doing what's expected. I don't know for certain, but I speculate they got in the habit of asking, *Is this [activity] essential to the business? Is it essential to our quality of life?* Using this simple filter, they said no to advertising. No to storewide sales. No to expansion, franchising, internet sales. Even the Bula website stayed pared down, with the bare minimum of information.

David and Yair applied the same principle of essentialism to their personal lives. Rather than upscaling their homes, for example, each stayed put in their original houses and made incremental upgrades over the years. They're still happily married to their first wives. They also decided, early on, not to have children. As they remarked often during our interviews, the decision proved pivotal to Bula's success. Remaining child-free removed a whole layer of financial worry from the equation and allowed them to focus more wholeheartedly on the business.

The wisdom of simplifying our lives has a distinguished history. Picasso defines art as the elimination of the unnecessary. Antoine de Saint-

Exupéry, author of *The Little Prince*, writes, "Perfection is achieved not when there's nothing to add, but when there's nothing left to take away." In their manual *The Elements of Style*, coauthors William Strunk Jr. and E. B. White admonish writers to omit needless words. And that's my cue to end this chapter. Here's to brevity.

In the Flow

"Happiness is in the flow of life."

ZENO, FOUNDER OF THE SCHOOL OF STOICISM

Surfers will tell you that the finest moments are those spent riding inside the hollow of the wave as the lip curls out and down into the trough. "Getting barreled" counts as surfing's ultimate maneuver, and surfers have coined dozens of admiring phrases to describe tube rides, including getting *shacked, pitted,* and *slotted.* Only a fraction of waves are both hollow and well shaped. Their rarity helps explain why tube riding is so fiendishly difficult to master. Less than 5 percent of surfers worldwide can place themselves inside the tube with any degree of consistency.[39]

For six years in a row, starting around 2012, Yair made an annual pilgrimage to Fiji to replenish his spirit and ride the premier waves off Tavarua Island. He described to me the exhilaration of those few seconds before he got shot out of the mouth of the tube. I imagine he entered a state of blissful flow, of total absorption, when he lost all track of time and the outside world.

Yair didn't just go to Fiji for the thrill of the wave riding. He lacked the typical egomania of a surfer possessed by the sport. True to character, Yair made friends with the locals. He won them over when he learned the language, mostly surf-related lingo, but it was his antics that endeared him most. Fijians do a haka, a ceremonial dance, before every rugby match. Yair took it upon himself to memorize the accompanying chant and would belt it out at opportune moments to the delight of the Fijians. Yair was such a crack-up, they gave him the nickname "The White Fijian."

Yair on a dreamy wave at Restaurants, a world-famous break in Fiji.

David on a surfing holiday in El Salvador.

While Yair was hamming it up in Fiji, David spelled him at Bula. Yair did the same for David when he went skiing in Utah or traveled to a popular surf break. Over the years, they'd worked out a pleasing, synchronized schedule. Except when one of them was away, they split the workday. David, more an early riser, opened the shop, and Yair came in at midday. Their shifts overlapped at lunch time. They'd catch up, and Yair would take the afternoon shift to closing time.

"Today I realized I typically put work in scare quotes, e.g., I've got to go to 'work' I think this is 50 percent because my work just isn't that serious. Running a surf shop isn't like being a heart surgeon in its significance. And 50 percent because I enjoy it so much that it rarely feels like true work."

DAVID TO MARCIA IN A WHATSAPP TEXT, MARCH 26, 2023

After years when both worked six or seven days a week, sharing all responsibilities, they eventually drew lines between their tasks, became specialists. This marked the start of Modern Bula, the era of their biggest lifestyle victory. They still put in grueling hours, but the work felt less and less like true work.

It's hard to overestimate the domino effect of their decisions. First, they went for quiet greatness, not flashy growth. Then, they gave each other the gift of a split workday. Finally, they learned how to play to each other's strengths.

"Bula's a Two-Legged Creature. It Needs Both Legs to Stand."

David: I actually enjoy negotiating with the suppliers, looking at past sales data, projecting the future year. You know, knocking things off the list. Yair's great at relationships. I kinda suck at the touchy-feely stuff, which is why Yair does 100 percent of the HR now. It used to be a disaster when I was involved. I feel I've improved, but I'm not at Yair's level.

Yair: And then the flip side of that, if I tried to do what Dave does, we'd pay 200 percent more for everything that we buy.

David: It's still hit or miss, but I've learned a lot from watching Yair deal with friendly but volatile young workers. I used to want to rebut stressful situations right away, like there was a chess clock ticking. There's a lot of strategic benefit in not being super reactive, which raises the tension. Yair has a more mellow leadership style, almost classically female, I guess.

Yair: Oh wow, I never realized that. I feel I interrupt people too much. I wish I could wait and listen more. If you let people talk, often they'll dig their way out of their own grave.

David: When I'm being a jerk, for example, Yair has a sensor. He knows to back off. He doesn't stoke the fire.

Yair: We've known each other so long, we balance each other out. I've had maybe two or three intense bouts of depression since we started Bula. I'm useless for weeks or months – however long it takes to come out of the hole. David stands by me and, without a word, picks up all the pressures of my nonfunctionality. In such close quarters, when one person's down, everybody feels it, even the employees.

David: Yair once compared managing employees to coaching a sports team. Even the best players can have a dip in form and even the most benighted can kick ass. They have mood swings, relationship breakups. Yair doesn't ignore it when employees have tantrums, but he likes to let the volatility play itself out.

Yair: David has super high standards. He can be demanding of employees and himself, which is what Bula needs to keep running smoothly. My default style is: "Sir, I see you just shoplifted from us. You must be going through difficult times. Would you like to talk about it? No, well, help yourself to more of the merchandise on the house. You probably need it more than I do."

David: That's not too much of an exaggeration! [laughter]

Yair: What else can I say? If it were just me running it on my own, or if I had partnered with someone just like me, the business would be a disorganized mess.

David: And if I was running Bula without Yair's mellowing influence, the business would flop just as badly, if not worse.

Yair: Yeah, Bula's a two-legged creature. It needs both legs to stand.

David: It takes the yin and the yang.

As David and Yair both openly admitted, Bula would have flopped if they were carbon copies of each other. For a little perspective on the topic of successful partnerships, we can turn to popular podcast host Guy Raz. In his book *How I Built This*, he cites many examples of business partners with different skills and compensating strengths.[40] Ben and Jerry. Warren Buffet and Charlie Munger. Wells and Fargo. Harley and Davidson. Although these cultural icons shared the same vision, and helped each other stay accountable to it, they didn't always think or act alike.

Again and again, we hear stories about entrepreneurial successes unlocked by founders who spark off each other's brilliance. As Raz points out, there's often a "bit of that fatefulness to [these stories]: the right idea in the right place, at the right time, with the right people."[41] His comment reminds me of the fateful first meeting of David and Yair, back in Art 101. When Yair took a seat next to David and struck up a casual conversation, he set in motion a chain of serendipitous events. That day in class, neither had a clue their easy camaraderie and friendly banter would serve them well as cofounders, but it's fun to look back and celebrate the moment.

23

Paradise Deserted

The pandemic shut down the entire island. Except for emergency flights, no jetliners landed at Queen Beatrix International Airport. The cruise ship docks emptied. No tourists queued up for lounge chairs at the beach or rolled expensive suitcases across the polished lobbies of the luxury hotels. The island's iconic *I Love Aruba* signs looked forlorn without visitors lining up for their photo op.

Aruba was deserted and cut off from the rest of the world. I imagine the sudden drop in population shifted the balance of power in favor of the island's diverse wildlife. The giant green iguanas (pronounced "u-wan-na" in Papiamento) could swim freely across the hotel swimming pools and relax in the miniature tropical forests, courtesy of resort developers. In the desert wilderness of Arikok National Park, wild goats could poke through the brush undisturbed by gawking visitors. With no noise pollution, the tropical mockingbird (*chuchubi*) could deliver melodious recitals, perched on the top of telephone wires, while the pretty troupial (*trupial*) yodeled and showed off its deep orange-red underbelly.

Normally, tourists outnumber locals by a ratio of seven to one. Aruba has one of the most tourism-dependent economies in the Caribbean. When the lockdown hit, locals in hospitality, service positions, and any job related to the tourist trade faced sudden hardship. Restaurants, schools, museums, casinos, hotels, and all manner of establishments suspended their activities during the initial phases of the pandemic. Overnight, it seemed, the Royal Plaza turned into a ghost town, overrun with vacancy signs and shuttered storefronts. Among the casualties was a Bula copycat, a touristy beachwear shop. Right before the pandemic, Bula's other direct competitor, Panache,

The troupial is one of more than 220 resident and migratory birds found in Aruba. Bubali Bird Sanctuary is a great place to spot its striking plumage. Photo credit: Sabrina Ernst, dreamstime.com.

Covid shuttered many shops in the Royal Plaza. Except for the sanitizer by the door, Bula's storefront looked unscathed.

had folded. The store never regained its mojo after the owners opened a second shop in the expensive hotel area.

At first, David and Yair were relieved, even jubilant, that two rivals had gone belly up one after the other. What an opportunity for Bula! But then they had second thoughts. Were the closures canaries in the coal mine?

During Covid, surfing pundits wrote gloomy editorials about the extinction of surf shops. Even before the pandemic, online retailers had been a looming threat. Now, with absolutely no one traveling to major surf breaks and all the scary economic uncertainties of 2020, who would want to buy surfboards, boardshorts, rash guards, and Yeti coolers?

"We Realized How Strong and Resilient We Were."

David: In the first eight weeks of the lockdown, it was like having a private island to ourselves. It would have been more beautiful and calming if we hadn't had an underlying feeling of doom. I remember driving across the island to Wariruri to go for a surf and not passing a *single* car, in either direction. It felt a little like living in a zombie movie.

Yair: At first we had to close Bula completely. Then we partially reopened by offering curbside pickup service. We'd run out with a mask on and hand packages to clients in their car. They were grateful and, like us, happy for any shred of normalcy, I think. When we reopened, we had limited hours. And there was a cap on the number of customers we could have in the store. Of course everyone had to be masked.

David: Our employees had to police the mask situation, which was often stressful and annoying. The locals returned to shopping, but not nearly as much as before because there was no back-to-school shopping. Many people were reluctant to leave their houses. It wasn't good for business for many months.

David and Dennis surfed every day as therapy during the Covid lockdown. Here, they're just coming out of the water at Wariruri.

Yair: The saving grace is Aruba is part of the Dutch kingdom. Holland was very generous with their financial aid, so few people lost their jobs. Bula participated in the paycheck assistance program, so none of our employees went without pay. Aruba does a good job with stuff like that. A lot of businesses didn't make it, though, because they were teetering before the pandemic. It was a panicky few months. We didn't know what we were dealing with, like everyone else.

David: I developed coping mechanisms so I wouldn't go nuts. I surfed every day for the first fifty days of the lockdown. The beaches were emptier than usual and more beautiful. When I wasn't worrying about the world ending, Aruba felt like a sanctuary, a small self-contained world.

A few weeks into the lockdown, I gave up coffee because it was making me anxious and jittery. I went cold turkey and drank tea instead. I got into pandemic cliché activities like meditation and baking sourdough bread. I experimented a lot with different types of flour and taught myself how to bake using the famous Tartine bakery's "Country Loaf" recipe.

Yair: I went into my utopian woodworking-fishing-surfing world. On day four of the lockdown, I sawed off the end of one of my fingers, and Ana had to rush me to the hospital late at night. We were worried the whole time the police would stop us. There were huge fines if you were caught on the road past curfew without the proper paperwork. So we were nervous about my bloody finger *and* the cops coming after us.

David: Even with the tip of his finger chopped off, Yair managed to make me an incredible Kumiko panel lamp for my birthday. It has a mid-century feel and a cool shell pattern.

Yair: I saw a guy on YouTube take a solid piece of wood and do intricate chiseling of the individual pieces at a precise angle with a jig. It looked unattainable at first, but I knew I had to learn how to do it. Kumiko is a Japanese method of assembling wooden pieces without using nails. You have all these individual pieces—squares or triangles or hexagons—and you build an intricate pattern. When you slide in the final piece, everything locks into place by pressure alone.

Yair built this Kumiko hanging liquor cabinet during his Covid staycation. The design on the left panel is cherry blossom; the right is sesame seed.

The repetition of making the same cut hundreds of times is super enjoyable for me. It's so concentrated, like tapping into an ancient process, and I can feel myself improve. Kumiko is an extreme, almost spiritual, example of "the whole is greater than the sum of the parts."

David: I put Yair's Kumiko panel in a central place in our living room. It reminds me of something good that came out of Covid.

Yair: When the restrictions were lifted, and we were able to open the shop full time, our new hours were 10 to 5. Some of our customers hated that because they work until five o'clock. But after eighteen years of working a 9:30 to 6:00 schedule, we chose to cut back.

David: The shorter hours didn't seem to hit our bottom line, amazingly. So yeah, we're never going back because of the quality of life it gives us.

Yair: That's the one concrete thing I remember from Covid. We realized how strong and resilient we were. It gave us confidence.

While David and Yair struggled to keep Bula afloat, Ana and Debbie navigated their own set of disruptions. Ana had to get creative when schools closed. As the founder and director of Beautiful Sun Montessori, the island's first dedicated Montessori school, she refused to cut any salaries (except her own) and gave parents a refund.

"I knew we couldn't just abandon the children and the families," she told me. "I asked myself, 'What would Mr. Rogers do?'" Ana developed her own special Zoom class like a television program. "It was fun and interactive," she reflected. "Like, I'd talk about shapes and ask the children to search around the house for the same shape. They were so proud to hold up their stuffed animal on the screen." The social connections were "so sweet," she said, "but it was really hard work."

During the lockdown, her anxieties grew, not just about losing her beloved school but also about all the suffering in the world. During the whole first year of Covid, she slept with her cat, Wolfgang, on her chest and practiced a lot of loving-kindness meditation.

Debbie wasn't particularly phased by Covid. "It was just what was happening at the time," she recalled. "I found this coffee at the grocery store I liked and realized it was, like, way more caffeinated than our usual grind. It made me so energetic, I knit a huge blanket while watching the series "'Grace and Frankie.'"

Pre-Covid, Debbie had taken a temporary teaching position. After years of tutoring kids one-on-one, she realized she loved classroom teaching. Early in the pandemic she decided to pursue a teaching career in earnest.

"I mean, we were locked down," she told me. "Why not use it as an opportunity to get my online teaching certification?" Debbie spent the next nine months earning her license and, soon afterward, landed a position as a math teacher at the International School of Aruba. Although Debbie didn't realize it at the time, she'd found her dream job.

At first, the Bula Four observed Aruba's strict social-distancing rules, but the forced separation didn't last long. They couldn't stand not seeing each other, so the two couples formed their own pod. They walked their dogs on the beach, had fish suppers on the patio, and rallied when Yair's beloved father died of Covid complications. He was Aruba's seventy-second fatality. It is one of those heartbreaking stories. No one could visit him in the hospital, not even Yair's mother, who got Covid at the same time. Yair had the unfortunate task of telling his mother, when she was strong enough, that her husband of fifty years had died.

What a strange, unsettling time that must have been. Even as the pandemic was taking lives and ravaging communities, the two couples couldn't go anywhere without feeling the pleasing warmth of the Aruban sun on their skin. The air smelled sweet from plumeria and tropical jasmine. Were they able to slow down and savor the beauty? Or did all the negatives swamp their attention?

"A small island is not just a place on a map; it's a psychological destination, a model of simplifying your life and making do with what is immediately on hand."[42]

THE SCHOOL OF LIFE

At Loyola University, Chicago psychologist Fred Bryant studies the reasons why we often spend more time counting our troubles than our blessings. As the inevitable result of evolution, humans tend to focus on the dangers in the environment. The threats can take our lives if we don't heed them, whereas the pleasures and joys don't clamor for our attention. From decades of study, Bryant has pinpointed why it's so hard to stop and notice what is wonderful about our lives.

"We're waiting for the next problem to arise," he said in a *Hidden Brain* podcast.[43] "And so we don't really immerse ourselves in the moment." The pleasures sometimes hide, he says. They require us to hunt and then spend time appreciating them. Bryant cites the many benefits of slowing down and "savoring" to combat the propensity of the mind to dwell on the negatives. Savoring is simply noticing something that's pleasurable, like a beautiful sunrise, a bite of chocolate, or the intoxicating fragrance of freshly baked bread. The essence of savoring, he tells us, is noticing a positive experience, whether it comes from outside or within us. By slowing down and paying attention, we can turn even the smallest of moments into an opportunity for enjoyment.

"So speed and impatience [are] really the enem[ies] of enjoyment. The lingering is the secret," Bryant observes.[44]

I don't know for certain, but I suspect the pandemic was an extreme mixed blessing for the Bula Four. Of course, there were all the stresses, and the emotional ups and downs, but they also got the benefit of a sabbatical. They used the luxury of time to work through their own life changes while supporting each other through it all. I can't imagine a more conducive place for savoring life's pleasures than a small island where the songbirds give recitals on the phone wires and the winds whip the waves into frothy peaks. The conditions may not be ideal for surfing, but they're perfect enough.

Bula Bags and Flying Fish for Christmas

Arubans love festive occasions. At Christmas, neighbors host open houses, put up elaborate decorations, and prepare lavish feasts. To sweeten the fun, a few Aruban families still boil cashew nuts and grind them with mounds of sugar to make *cashupete*, a traditional beverage served as a holiday treat.

Each year, thousands of Christmas trees get imported into this tiny Caribbean isle. In recent times, a new ritual has surfaced: a blue Bula bag under every tree. Kimberly Rooijakkers is credited with spotting the trend. Kimberly owns and runs Boardwalk Hotel, a tucked-away boutique resort opposite the Ritz Carlton.

When I requested a short interview, Kimberly said yes right away. We arranged to meet in the lobby, a sun-drenched room with tall windows, creamy coral-stone tiles, and a welcoming Caribbean decor. I had just settled into a high-backed rattan chair when Kimberly walked toward me. She was already smiling, her hand outstretched. I was surprised at how rested she looked. Together with her twin sister, Kimberly had recently finished an exhaustive renovation of the hotel.

Kimberly took me on a private tour of the grounds, a former coconut plantation. We wound our way through a manicured jungle of towering palms, lush tropical plants, and hidden nooks with hammocks for the guests. She walked ahead of me at a fast clip, speaking the whole time and pointing out the sights. Guest casitas dotted the landscape in shades of sky blue, tangerine, and lemony yellow. Occasionally Kimberly would greet a guest or a member of her staff. Everyone looked happy to be there.

Boardwalk Hotel is a calm oasis for weary travelers.

Like Bula, Boardwalk Hotel has that ability to make you feel right at home, instantly and seemingly without effort.

A few minutes into our walking tour, I popped the question.

"So what's the story about the Bula bags under the Christmas tree?"

"Well, it's a fact," she said, without a second's hesitation. Kimberly seemed surprised that I wanted proof. "I see the bags everywhere I go, filled with gifts large and small," she added. "The shop has this magnetism that pulls the community to it."

As an enterprising business owner, Kimberly had studied Bula's DNA for years as part of her fascination with the Small Giants Community started by Bo Burlingham and his cofounder, Paul Spiegelman. In 2016, Burlingham authored the book *Small Giants: Companies That Choose to Be Great Instead of Big.* That book had a huge impact on Kimberly's vision for her business.

"It's really tough for entrepreneurs when they decide to stay small because they have to be on top of everything," she said, turning to look at me. "You have to fight growing bigger and becoming average. Bula could have franchised, set up shops all over the world, but they stuck to their core value of having fun and doing something a little outrageous. David and Yair have such a good eye for appealing to their core market."

Kimberly paused to jot down a note. We'd just walked past a palm whose yellowing fronds needed a trim. I got the sense Kimberly was multitasking all the time. She walked ahead of me toward the pool.

"I'm not that close with David and Yair," she continued, "but I know Bula fits the definition of a small giant." We watched a couple slide noiselessly into the big pool and then splash at each other like kids. "Out of all the surf shops in the world, Bula has developed its own authentic brand," Kimberly continued. "They're still small, still innovating. They constantly amaze us."

We said our goodbyes back in the lobby. As I was leaving, the woman at the reception desk beamed at me. She looked so friendly, I briefly wondered if we had met before. There was that eerie connection you sometimes feel with a perfect stranger.

I was psyched to tell David and Yair about my interview, but I didn't get a chance until later. The Christmas season is Bula's busiest, with lines out the door. David and Yair always bring in extra staff to handle the crush of shoppers and the gift wrapping. Every day is a flat-out marathon, and Christmas 2022 was no exception.

Scenes of tranquility at the Boardwalk Hotel.

"An Embarrassment of Riches"

David: The Christmas vibe was really great, really solid. It was our first one, post-Covid, where we didn't have to enforce masks or limit the number of people in the store.

Yair: Yeah, it was incredibly busy, even more than usual at Christmas, probably because there was pent-up shopping energy from the pandemic.

David: That Christmas was especially fun. We'd developed a kind of looseness . . . a friendly, back-slapping casualness. I'd say it was our best yet, money wise, and in terms of enjoyment.

Yair: Yeah, there was this parade of Bula bags leaving the store. But sometimes it felt awkward encountering other business owners in the area who were struggling—it was like an embarrassment of riches.

David: We were cognizant that Bula was closing in on twenty years in business. It amazed us we were doing so well when so many other shops were struggling or going out of business.

Yair: On Christmas Day, our day off, I always get to chill out and reflect on how things are going. I like to go fishing. Fishing clears the mind.

True to tradition, Yair spent Christmas Day 2022 at sea. Frank Kelly, a local artist and Bula regular, joined him for the occasion, as he often did. When Frank's income sources dwindled during Covid, Yair had proposed an idea.

"Let's fish together," he suggested. "You help me out with the boat, and we'll split the catch." The weekly supply of fresh fish sustained Frank's family during the pandemic, and the two of them became friends. On slow fishing days, Yair would compose songs with lengthy lyrics, accompanied by Frank's mimicking of trumpets and drums. Whenever they caught a big fish, they'd hug, shout, and sing.

Frank, affectionately known as Taki, is one of several local artists David and Yair befriended over the years. Bula pays artists a royalty in exchange for the use of their artwork. The exposure helps them out while adding spice to Bula's constantly evolving house brands.

At Yair's urging, Taki taught himself how to make gyotaku prints. In Japanese, *gyo* means fish; *taku* means impression. The ancient method started before the invention of cameras as a way to record the species and size of trophy fish. Gyotaku has since evolved into a popular art form. Artists rub the fish with nontoxic paint and make an impression with rice paper. It takes considerable care and skill to capture the anatomical details of the fish, and no two prints are exactly alike.

Taki models the limited-edition Bula T inspired by his gyotaku fish print.

"Most surf shops are pretty clueless about stuff like this," David explained. "They essentially stock the same merchandise the surf industry tells them to. We pride ourselves on being a little more creative . . . and really down with the community."

During our interview, Kimberly had echoed a similar point. "Bula's support of local artists has brought the pride of Aruba alive," she told me. "It's the same spirit that started when David and Yair came out with the first *Dushi yiu!* shirt."

Yair found inspiration for yet another iconic Bula T when a flying fish lost its way and dropped into the boat on Christmas day.

"We did a little dance and slapped each other on the back," Taki recalled. "When Yair asked me to make a print of the fish for a new Bula shirt, I couldn't wait to get started."

In Papiamento, flying fish are called *buladó*, which simply means "flier." "It's so cool the name of the flying fish contains the word Bula," Yair told me. "It's fun to play on that. For obvious reasons, we've adopted the flying fish as Bula's spirit animal."

With a powerful thrust of their tails, flying fish get airborne to escape predators in the sea. The fish can glide for up to 650 feet using their highly modified pectoral fins as wings. Once in the air, though, they risk becoming prey for frigates and other predatory birds. And if they dive to evade attack from above, they can fall victim to tuna, mahi-mahi, blue marlin, and other large fish.

Yair told me he always loves seeing flying fish when he's out fishing. When I asked why, he paused.

"I guess it's because it's an animal that really shouldn't exist—a fish that flies out of its element, just like Bula," he said.

"What do you mean?"

"Bula shouldn't be the success it is. We've always done things counter to conventional wisdom. Somehow it's worked."

I couldn't let Yair's understatement just sit there. Enough with the no-claiming rule! As soon as I had the chance, I circled back on WhatsApp and asked him what he was most proud of as Bula's co-owner.

Yair didn't make me wait long for his answer: Staying best friends with David was number one, he texted, followed closely by thriving for nearly two decades in a declining retail environment worldwide.

After months and months of interviews, that's about as close as Yair ever got to claiming Bula's remarkable twenty-year run.

25

Who Moved the Cake?

I was about to book my flight to Aruba when I got a WhatsApp message from David suggesting I nix my travel plans. He was polite about encouraging me to steer clear of Bula's twentieth-anniversary celebration. He's always polite. And caring. I don't know anyone who is more thoughtful about other people's feelings. Still, I wish I could have been there.

That party was a funny thing. Originally David and Yair threatened what they called a Bula Bash. There was discussion of hosting a shindig in Yair's backyard with a blow-up play set, live music, drinks, and a catered dinner. And, of course, a birthday cake. David and Yair seemed seriously gung-ho about celebrating the milestone. But, as the day neared, the wobbly legs of the Bula Bash started to collapse. Unsurprisingly, the introverted surf shop owners got cold feet about hosting a showy party, essentially in their own honor.

Unplugged from the original party concept, David and Yair scrambled to pull something together in the limited time remaining. The actual occasion was perfect in its own low-key, sweet way. A last-minute invitation went out with the promise of free beer and live music at the shop. David and Yair had invited Toto Boroto, an Aruban-born musician and artist visiting from Paris, to play electric guitar. Hillary and Jeff Arnold, David's close friends from Charleston, South Carolina, performed crowd pleasers from their nightclub repertoire, including a jazzy rendition of the Dee Dee Warwick favorite, "You're No Good." At some point during the party, a Bula fan showed up with his guitar, and the others made room for him in the tight space between the clothing displays.

Happy 20th birthday, Bula!

Drop by for smiles, stories, beers, and live music by Toto Boroto from 3-5pm today.

The morning of the shindig, a friendly invitation went out on social media to thousands of Bula fans around the world.

"It was funny because there wasn't a stage set up," Jeff told me. "We were just sitting on chairs they brought from the back room."

"Yeah, we were a very eclectic group," Hillary added. "It was a fun challenge to play with people we'd never met."

Taki, Yair's fishing buddy, paid his respects by serving home-brewed rum drinks, frosty beers, and tropical juices he'd squeezed earlier that day. The scent of passion fruit and pineapple wafted through the air, mingling with the coconut overtones of freshly opened surf wax. I imagine the shop smelled like a piña colada on a perfect beach day. David and Yair toggled between their roles as party hosts and surf-shop owners. The tourists who wandered into the shop at first felt like gatecrashers at a family reunion, but many of them ended up staying for drinks and pastechis.

The partygoers exclaimed over the two miniature greyhounds that wandered in with Ash, one of the original Bula crew. He'd opened a boutique, Tangerine, right next door. Ash grew up in a family of seamstresses and upholsterers, but it was his unofficial degree from Bula University that nudged him to open his own two-human, two-dog operation. He turns out artful handcrafted canvas bags and accessories influenced by a traditional nautical style. When I asked him for his impressions of Bula's twentieth, he took his time to find the right words.

"It was just very relaxed and happy," he said, after a lengthy reflection. "They're [David and Yair] the biggest blessing. . . . I learned most of everything at Bula about business, right? I can create, but I'm not a businessperson. Now I've got more money coming in than going out. I've got my freedom."

*Tico and King, Ash's greyhounds, tag along
with him wherever he goes.*

The laid-back party vibe Ash described took a more serious turn when the cake appeared on the scene. Per Bula tradition, employees in Bula T-shirts paraded an Aruban-style butter cake, topped with glistening fresh fruit, toward the center island. Spontaneously, the pickup band of musicians belted out a slightly discordant rendition of "Happy Birthday." Everyone sang. David and Yair proudly took their positions by the cake, as they've done every year since 2004, and blew out all the candles in perfect unison.

Someone captured the proud moment in a video. The clip shows the moment David puts his arm awkwardly around Yair. As the strains of "Happy Birthday, Dear Bula," play on, they make jokes and kid each other. Overhead, a giant blue "20" helium balloon floats amid the surfboards suspended from the ceiling.

The cake disappeared, never to make another appearance. On good authority I learned David had whisked it to the back room. Apparently, he didn't like the idea of guests, in various stages of inebriation, leaving a trail of cake crumbs and goo on the merchandise.

When I asked Ana what she thought of the event, she bubbled over with enthusiasm, describing it as a "party for someone who doesn't really like to tell people that it's their birthday or make a big deal out of it, but are secretly pleased when friends remember and a nice, little gathering happens."

Ana and Debbie checked in with each other during the party, as friends do. Debbie was the one who hunted down the cake and made sure the electric guitarist and a few others went home with nice-sized portions.

"I know what it's like when you *really* want to eat cake," Debbie said, laughing.

Ash told me he was surprised David and Yair allowed a cake in the shop at all.

"We always had it outside or in someone's house," he said. "They've gotten more flexible."

*Cado got swept off his feet at Bula's
anniversary celebration.*

If you scour Bula's photo archives, you can time travel back to cake ceremonies from 2004 onward. It's pretty much the same scenario: the employees crowd around, beaming, as David and Yair ooh and aah. As the years tick by, David and Yair get older, but the employees magically stay young. David typically acts out a bit, making a funny face or pointing with pretend seriousness at something off-camera. Yair shrugs, pretending to be shocked at David's antics. In every photo you can tell how immensely proud they are, standing side by side, reveling in the dream.

Final Words

Bula Surf Shop: four parts beach culture, two parts artsy, two parts core ocean activities. Shake well.

You both left impressive careers, moved to a small island in the Caribbean, and started a small surf shop. After twenty years, I'm curious if the smallness or predictability ever gets to you?

David: I've never had a static feeling. We're always burning the chaff, moving toward consistency. I get pleasure from seeing the new surfboards come in. I love tinkering with the design of a new T-shirt and helping to build the Bula culture. No, there's never a feeling of being bored with it.

Yair: We have fun and figure things out together every day. Even solving the little things can be very satisfying. Of course, in a small space, if someone is having a bad day, it rubs off on everyone else. And let's say if we have to let an employee go, then everyone and his uncle knows about it. It's such a close-knit community.

You started Bula in your twenties. In the photos, you look so young and incredibly earnest. To what extent has that youthful passion faded for you?

David: I suppose it's like a romantic infatuation that's matured but never completely disappeared. I recently read a *New Yorker* article by Paul McCartney where he wrote about all the small coincidences that had to happen to make the Beatles. He used the word "magic" to describe it. There's one passage I really like: "It's one of those wonderful life lessons about saying yes when life presents these opportunities to you. You never know where they might lead." Of course, Bula is no Beatles, but I still feel the same way about our little project that Paul does about his. The magic's still there. Who knows where Bula will take us next?

Yair: Just because you've done something for a long time, it doesn't mean you can't enjoy it. I kind of enjoy the repetition. In the low season, we get to think about what new things we can do. In the high season, when it's busy all the time, we can't wait to get back to the low season again. Retail is changing constantly. There's always variety in terms of brands and industry trends.

David: Retail's a simple thing, relatively speaking, but there's a satisfaction in looking back at what we've learned about the nuances of customer service and ordering merchandise and all the rest. I'm sure the omelet chef in the documentary *Jiro Dreams of*

Sushi felt the same when he finally cooked a decent egg after ten years and graduated to toasting seaweed.

Bula started as a low-key experiment that would probably fail. Many entrepreneurs set out with their guns blazing. What kept you motivated?

David: Well, the experimental aspect gave us the freedom to fail. Especially at first, neither of us had a clue what we were doing. We had to learn everything the hard way. It was all new and pretty exciting. We made a series of small bets. If we had aimed too high, we would have had that much farther to fall.

Yair: If we have any strengths in our business model, it's that we make adjustments. You know, the test-and-learn philosophy. We may not be the greatest at coming up with good ideas, but we're quick to get rid of the bad ones. And when we land on a really good idea, we hold onto it for all it's worth.

Okay, I get that you never had the reach-for-the-stars ambition of many entrepreneurs. How do you explain your success? You've obviously succeeded beyond your wildest dreams.

David: What comes to mind is that customer service mantra about under promising and over delivering. That's what we have always tried to do with Bula, and there are parallels to life in general. If you set reasonable expectations, as the Stoics often said, you're happy when you meet or exceed them.

Yair: Yeah, I agree, but there was that one period in 2010–2011 when we ordered way too much inventory. After several years of incredible growth, we had bought into our own invincibility. We had boxes and boxes of boardshorts upstairs, just sitting there. It took us several months to sell off the excess inventory. After the dust settled, we reminded ourselves why we started Bula in the first place . . . you know, our purpose. We had always wanted to have a business where we could earn a decent salary and enjoy life. We never wanted to get on the hamster wheel of blindly chasing growth, quarter after quarter. Even when sales hit the wall in 2010–2011, we never really worried we'd go out of business. We were still profitable and having a good time, most days.

David: Right, but I can see why some people might accuse us of lacking ambition. Definitely my grandmother in Palm Beach did. She never lost hope I'd come to my senses and go back into law. I think it really comes down to what you're ambitious about. If you're ambitious for a happy life with friends you love and a job you find rewarding, then I'd say we set ourselves a pretty high bar.

Rich people can get obsessive about their money. Even though they're extremely well off, they worry about every penny, the cost of groceries, the cost of coffee, property taxes. They're afraid of losing what they have or they obsess about what they don't have. You both drive cars with lots of mileage. You live in the same houses you bought years ago. You work in the same space. You're still married to the same wives [laughter]. Do you ever get the urge to break bad or spend extravagantly?

David: Well, neither of us have this burning ambition to acquire things. If we did, we would have opened up in other locations. We would have expanded, so we could make more money and get bigger and bigger. If I won the lottery, I can't think of what I'd do differently. Maybe replace my rusted-out, old beachmobile? That's a boring answer. . . .

Yair: Yeah, it really frees you up when you have no mortgage and no debt. I am much happier than I imagined I could ever be. The business itself is inherently interesting. The personal relationships, not just with David but with employees and clients, are satisfying. But also, equally if not more, Bula is the means to the end of living a life we enjoy.

That's a really interesting point. Many people consider a financially successful business their end goal. Say more.

Yair: I remember this one time at David's house. Ana and I went over to David's for Monday night dinner, as usual. I brought over wahoo, and we grilled it. Ana told a story about Kurt Vonnegut and Joseph Heller. She'd just read an article about them meeting up on Nantucket at some multimillionaire's house.

Apparently, Vonnegut turned to Heller at dinner and asked: "How does it feel to have dinner in the house of someone who makes more in one day than all the royalties combined of all the books you've ever written?"

Heller replied, "I have one thing this guy doesn't have. Knowledge that I have more than enough." Heller's statement is the closest I have to a religion . . . other than that button we sell at Bula. It *totally* sums up my philosophy of life [laughing].

David: Right! At Bula, we reduce centuries of philosophy to five words on the head of a pin.

Do you ever get a sneak attack of FOMO (the Fear of Missing Out)?

Yair: Sometimes, but not really. A few years ago, I ran into a college professor of mine at a party. She was, like, my idol, a very charismatic person. She trained to be an astronaut and then decided to be a marine biologist. I worked in her lab as a graduate student. At this party I went to, she asked me what I was up to, and I told her I ran a surf shop in Aruba. She said, "Wow, that's really interesting," which I interpreted (right or wrong) as insincere. She probably wondered why she had wasted her time writing my letter of recommendation to Yale.

David: I really like the reverse idea of JOMO (the Joy of Missing Out). You know, all the bullets I've dodged. Why wouldn't I be grateful for all the sucky jobs I didn't take, the toxic cultures I avoided, and the control freaks I didn't get stuck working for?

Yair: When I tell people we run a surf shop, they almost always say, *Awesome*, initially. The more materialistic people wonder, can you really make a living doing that? I agree with David. If I won the lottery, I wouldn't go out and buy a bigger boat or a different house. I do wish I could get a microchip implemented where I, like, don't require sleep. I'd do more fishing, more surfing, more woodworking. I'm not looking for anything else.

David fishes while Yair sails the larger of the two sailboats he built by hand in his workshop. The project consumed Yair for three years, a true labor of love.

David: This is kinda off the point, but the happiest people I know actually like the work they do. They'd do it even if they didn't have to worry about money. Everyone's so different though.

Okay, here's a big one: What has Bula given you?

Yair: Time and flexibility. I can come home and go straight back to my workshop. I've never thought of myself as a creative type, but it turns out I have a certain knack for woodworking. Several summers in a row, I went to classes at the WoodenBoat School in Maine. I learned how to make my first small sailboat, then a bigger one. Now I'm making guitars. I'm obsessed. I tiptoe out of the bedroom after Ana goes to sleep and go back to the workshop until late at night.

David: All we ever wanted was a sustainable livelihood. We don't have children by choice. Kids would have definitely changed the formula. We never had to worry about paying college tuition. Bula has freed me from constantly worrying about money. Why would I want to mess this up?

For David's forty-eighth birthday, Yair made him a ukulele
out of mango wood. He's since taught himself how to make
a variety of custom guitars, each a functional work of art.

Yair: I don't mean to downplay the importance of Bula as the engine of our happiness. The business has given us a pleasant, satisfying life. But come on, look at where we live. The color of the water, it's hypnotizing. The climate is pretty much perfect. It's never too hot, because the breeze cools things off. After Covid, I lost that desire to travel. I feel oddly content. Some people just can't wait to go somewhere else. I'm the opposite of that. I mean, if this isn't enough, then what the hell is going to be enough?

David and Yair chose to remain child free, but they
outfitted huge numbers of future wave riders

David: Right, we have what people often work years to get: Free time, tropical weather, short commutes, interesting work. I feel bad about friends who toiled away after law school, doing corporate discovery work and telling paralegals what to do. They get a three-week allotment of freedom each year . . . that's just not a good ratio over the span of a short lifetime.

What's it like to age in place, so to speak, as two surfers running a surf shop? Surfing is such a youth-obsessed sport.

Yair: Dave and I are getting old, right? I mean, not old old, but we're in our late forties. So we may like a certain style of clothing that's reminiscent of a cool period in the '80s or '90s, but it's hideous to young kids.

David: Remember that Rolling Stones–inspired shirt design I labored over? The employees took one look and said, No way. They hadn't even heard of the Rolling Stones. It was, like, ancient history to them. That humiliation has stuck with me. As a coping mechanism, I've adopted the *Beach Til I Die* philosophy [laughter].

Yair:　David came up with the idea to put that expression on T-shirts. They've sold really well.

What does *Beach Til I Die* mean to you, exactly?

Yair:　It's like saying, "I'm such a chill guy. I'm going to surf until I die. I'll never get jaded."

David:　Right, it's kinda cheesy and fun . . . a take on the self-conscious, self-aware language of the surf industry. *Beach Til I Die* plays on the idea surfers never get old because they're always focused on riding the next wave. They're always honing and perfecting.

One word for your friendship?

Yair:　Unwavering.
David:　Brothers.

Ana (masked by her black hat) joins David and
Yair in a champagne toast to good friends, fair winds,
and new journeys.

Epilogue

Just when you thought you'd seen the last of Bula Surf Shop and its cofounders, there's a new chapter in the making. After twenty-one years in the Royal Plaza Mall, Bula has packed up and left the premises. Not because of financial or cofounder difficulties, thankfully. The Royal Plaza had struggled, like many malls, so when a local condo developer bought the property, Bula and the other tenants found new digs. David and Yair never dreamed of relocating to a sleek building by the harbor, just a hop and a skip from Bula's original home, but that's what fate had in store for them.

The new retail space needed a total overhaul, from its unfinished floor to the exposed ceiling. David and Yair threw themselves into all the messy details of the construction project while running Bula as they always have. True to form, Yair went into full woodworking mode, taking precise measurements, importing cedar for the walls, and building all manner of custom fixtures.

The renovations consumed them for months until, finally, it was time to flip the switch. David and Yair chose Monday, March 4, 2024, as the official move date because Bula was closed on Sunday, and that gave them the chance to hustle all the merch across the street and set up in one day. It was another all-hands-on-deck push, not unlike their stealth move next door in 2008. As before, employees past and present worked their tails off, among them Astor, Bula's beloved Mr. Green Eyes. Heartwarmingly, several friends also lent a hand. Frank "Taki" Kelly, whom you remember from chapter 24, toted heavy boxes for days, and Marvin, a fellow surfer and dentist, baked an enormous bread pudding that kept everyone fired up and fueled.

Yair showed up on opening day, but barely. After exerting himself for months, he had a debilitating flare-up of Crohn's and ended up rushing back and forth to the emergency room for IV drips and painkillers.

"The last two weeks before the move got totally crazy," he told me. "I didn't sleep much. The weekend we started moving merchandise into the shop, I had a total burnout."

I had grave concerns about Yair's health, of course, but also about Bula. Would Bula's move to a bigger and fancier location prove its undoing? The thought of the shop overextending itself and losing its "Purpleness" made me queasy, almost seasick. I wallowed in worries for a couple of days, then reached out to David and Yair.

"The new store feels different," Yair told me. "It's breathing a lot of new life into people's work ethic."

David added that they had rewarded each member of the Bula crew with a massage at Manchebo Spa, proving that some things never change. They're still pampering the hell out of their employees.

Without a word from me, David addressed the giant in the room: Was the new space maybe a tad too big, too slick?

"My observation is that the new space is more of what we love," he said. "There's more organic light, more glass, and sunshine coming into the shop. We're right by the water, with a tiny little beach right out the front door, and it's nice to be closer to the water . . . which is what we're all about."

"Yeah, we've got more room for stuff," Yair added , "but it's never going to be some big, gigantic store. There's still the feeling of a small community space."

Looking at the photos of the beautiful new Bula, I was struck by one in particular. David and Yair are working side by side at the wooden center island Yair designed and built by hand. The register is in the perfect place, next to where the T-shirts hang, exactly the way Yair planned it. They both look utterly focused, almost rapt, in the flow of the moment.

Which makes me think: Big dreams are thrilling, but small moments are almost better. Whether it's planting a garden, opening a sushi shop, or playing an instrument, we can experience joy when our struggles end and we get something right, or at least as close to right as humanly possible. Anyone who's ever made anything knows that good, honest creative work will always surprise us—as long as we remain open to the unexpected.

This book taught me it's no use waiting for inspiration to appear at a distance. I stepped forward, receptive and curious, and David and Yair met me halfway, giving me perspectives I couldn't unsee. I put down a word, and another word, until it was time to sleep and then repeat the same thing the next day. I kept going because I didn't want to let anyone down, least of all myself.

I've always hesitated to take up space, emotionally and physically. Rather than speak out, I'm more likely to make myself small, origami tight. Writing this book opened up a new transformative space for me with doors opening and light pouring in through big open windows. I was *in it*—immersed and dedicated. I was really *doing i*t. And no one was going to stop me. Luckily, I had the gift of escapism that comes from walking around in somebody else's world for long stretches at a time. I got to witness David and Yair struggle, see them rise, and earn their happiness. Somewhere along the path, I found my own happiness as a byproduct of committing, wholeheartedly, to something bigger than my own petty preoccupations.

It took me a very long time to wake up to this truth. Which makes me think of something else. Coming-of-age stories are supposed to take place in our youth, but I feel like I've just started blooming. Now, how cool is that?

Endnotes

1. Austin Kleon, *Show Your Work! 10 Ways to Share Your Creativity and Get Discovered* (New York: Workman, 2014), p. 185.
2. Josh Howarth *Startup Failures Rate Statistics,* Exploding Topics, November 3, 2023.
3. Ibid.
4. Vivek H. Murthy, *Together: The Healing Power of Human Connection in a Sometimes Lonely World,* (New York: Harper Wave, 2020), p. 13.
5. Ibid.
6. Robin Dunbar, *Friends: Understanding the Power of Our Most Important Relationships* (London: Little, Brown, 2021), p. 203.
7. Jeffrey A. Hall, "How Many Hours Does It Take to Make a Friend?" *Journal of Social and Personal Relationships,* 36:4 (April 2019), pp. 1278–1296.
8. Shankar Vedantam, Rhaina Cohen, Thomas Lu, Tara Boyle, Parth Shah, Cat Schuknecht, "Playing Favorites: When Kindness Toward Some Means Callousness Toward Others," June 8, 2020, in *Hidden Brain,* produced by National Public Radio, podcast, 54:00, https://www.npr.org/2020/06/05/870352402/playing-favorites-when-kindness-toward-some-means-callousness-toward-others.
9. Rona Caster, *Island Life: Aruba's Best-Kept Diary* (English Version, Media Minds Communication, cosponsored by UNOCA, based on the author's *Island Life* column from 1992 to 2004), p. 136.
10. Alain de Botton, *The Pleasures and Sorrows of Work* (New York: Vintage International, 2009), p. 277.
11. Matt Warshaw, *The Encyclopedia of Surfing* (New York: Harcourt, 2005), p. 577.
12. Guy Raz, *How I Built This: The Unexpected Paths to Success from the World's Most Inspiring Entrepreneurs* (Boston: Houghton Mifflin Harcourt, 2020), p. 50.
13. Chuck Klosterman, *The Nineties: A Book* (New York: Penguin Books, 2022), p. 24.
14. Adam Grant (@AdamGrant), "Following your passion is a luxury," Twitter, September 13, 2022, 1:02 p.m., https://twitter.com/AdamMGrant/status/1569733211294691330.
15. Terri Trespicio, *Unfollow Your Passion: How to Create a Life that Matters to You* (New York: Simon & Schuster, 2021), pp. 100–101.
16. Warshaw, p. 140.
17. Warshaw, p. 581.
18. Seth Godin, *Purple Cow: Transform Your Business by Being Remarkable* (New York: Penguin Books, 2005), p. 108.
19. Malcolm Gladwell, *Outliers: The Story of Success* (New York: Little, Brown, 2008), p. 149.
20. "Friendship: Close Ties That Enhance, Extend Life," CBS Sunday Morning, March 17, 2013, reported by Rita Braver https://www.cbsnews.com/news/friendship-close-ties-that-enhance-extend-life/.
21. Ibid.
22. Dunbar, p. 274.
23. Geoffrey Greif, *Buddy System: Understanding Male Friendships* (London: Oxford University Press, 2008).
24. Kate Leaver, *The Friendship Cure: Reconnecting in the Modern World* (New York: The Overlook Press, 2018), p. 96.
25. Raz, p. 116.

26. Shankar Vedantam, "The Snowball Effect," March 1, 2021, in *Hidden Brain,* produced by National Public Radio, podcast, 1:02:27, https://hiddenbrain.org/podcast/the-snowball-effect/

27. Godin, *Purple Cow,* p. 40.

28. Malcolm Gladwell, *The Tipping Point: How Little Things Can Make a Big Difference* (New York: Little, Brown, 2000), quote on jacket cover.

29. Raz, p.206.

30. "Daniel Lubetzky: On a Mission to Spread Kindness," January 9, 2023, in *Clear and Vivid,* hosted by Alan Alda, podcast, 41:02, https://clear-vivid-with-alan-alda.simplecast.com/episodes/daniel-lubetsky-on-a-mission-to-spread-kindness.

31. Raz, p. 255.

32. Jennifer Senior, "It's Your Friends Who Break Your Heart," *The Atlantic,* February 9, 2022. https://www.theatlantic.com/magazine/archive/2022/03/why-we-lose-friends-aging-happiness/621305/.

33. Gladwell, *Outliers,* pp. 19–20.

34. Adam Grant and Esther Perel, "Relationships at Work with Esther Perel," July 19, 2021, *Work Life with Adam Grant,* produced by TED Audio Collective, podcast, 1:09:16.

35. Gladwell, *Outliers,* p. 11.

36. Shankar Vedantum, Tara Boyle, Brigid McCarthy, Annie Murphy Paul, Laura Kwerel, Kristin Wong, Ryan Katz, Autumn Barnes, and Andrew Cadwick, "Do Less," June 6, 2022, in *Hidden Brain,* produced by Hidden Brain Media, podcast, 1:00:27, https://hiddenbrain.org/podcast/do-less.

37. Guy Raz, "Patagonia: Yvon Chouinard," December 15, 2017, in *How I Built This With Guy Raz,* produced by National Public Radio, podcast, 28:00. https://www.npr.org/2018/02/06/572558864/patagonia-yvon-chouinard.

38. Vedantam, "Do Less."

39. Warshaw, p. 654.

40. Raz, p. 44.

41. Ibid.

42. Alain de Botton, ed., *Small Pleasures* (School of Life Press, Penguin, 2016), p. 17.

43. Shankar Vedantam, Brigid McCarthy, Annie Murphy Paul, Kristin Wong, Laura Kwerel, Ryan Katz, Autumn Barnes, Andrew Chadwick, "You 2.0: Slow Down!," August 21, 2023, in *Hidden Brain,* produced by Hidden Brain Media, podcast, 55:50, https://hiddenbrain.org/podcast/you-2-0-slow-down/.

44. Ibid.

Acknowledgments

Matt, it only seemed right to dedicate the book to you. When I couldn't face another minute at the keyboard, I'd take a walking holiday. Chugging up the steep hill to the Wagner farm, I'd call you, breathless and consumed by writerly doubts. I'll never forget the time you cut me off, mid-whine. "Mom, you've gone this far, why not keep going?" Yes, exactly. That's exactly what I needed to do.

Everlasting gratitude to David Putnam and Yair Lichtenstein, the book's reluctant heroes. Good guys that they are, they indulged me the privilege of pulling up a chair and saying, *Okay, I want to hear everything*. I returned continually to them for insights about their friendship, Aruban customs, Bula's history, and surfing lore. They patiently edited my hilariously inauthentic attempts at mimicking the lingo of hardcore surfers. All my factory-recall early drafts got an intense poring over, too. I can't imagine more creative, discerning, or kind collaborators.

Platinum-level thanks to their wives, Debbie Kunder and Ana von Saalfeld, for sharing their personal memories, archival photos, and big-picture impressions. Every page is better for their contributions.

For a multilayered view of Bula and its cofounders, I relied on interviews with close friends, longtime employees, and local businesspeople. Everyone I interviewed, often more than once, seemed inordinately happy to talk about what Bula has meant to them. Immense thanks to: Ashlin Ahlip, Ricardo "Cado" de Lannoy, Dennis Schoneveld, Greg Lucas, Ervin Anaya, Maurice Neme, Kimberly Rooijakkers, Sarah-Quita Offringa, Frank "Taki" Kelly, Georgina Bustamante, Rona Caster, and Hillary and Jeff Arnold.

Shelley Sperry, the book's editorial adviser, coached me out of a major funk. A year into the project, I brought her a lumpy, misshapen draft. I was so discouraged, I'd lost the fire to finish. Shelley gently urged me to step back and begin again. With her help, I was able to build the inner scaffolding the book so sorely needed. To call her a miracle worker is no exaggeration.

I am grateful to the book's early readers: Sally Chapman, William Parkhurst, Alan Fishman, Marcie Bronstein, Michelle Patterson, Elana Kupor, Beth Kallman Werner, and Katie Bannon, who educated me on the finer points of world building. What an astute, supportive group you all are.

Writing this book has skyrocketed my appreciation for my forever friends: Lisa Kelly, Trisha Derr, Jacque Rochester, Carol Ardell, and Sally Jaskold, who doubled as the book's expert copy editor and fact checker. I adore and admire you all.

Heartfelt thanks, always, for the bedrock support of my sisters and brothers and our extended family: the Blasers, Capuanos, Chapmans, Putnams, and Speranzas. I am supremely lucky to live out my days in your company.

Finally, my deepest bow to David, my husband and partner in life. Where would I be without you? I shudder to think how much less of a book this would have been without your loving prods and admonishments. You are my bridge to a life of constant adventure, and I'm forever smitten.

In fifth grade, **Marcia Heath** published a class newsletter investigating a friend's lost diamond ring—a genuine fake—and other mysteries of school life. The storytelling instinct stuck. After decades as a publicist at Simon & Schuster, executive editor at Harcourt, and corporate brand strategist, she was still crafting other people's stories when a random conversation under a mango tree sparked her first book. *Little Giant*, her award-winning biography, solves the riddle of how two unlikely entrepreneurs defied the odds to build a dream life in the Caribbean. Marcia lives in Midcoast Maine with her husband and their overly affectionate Boykin Spaniel. Connect at https://littlegiantbook.com

www.ingramcontent.com/pod-product-compliance
Lightning Source LLC
Chambersburg PA
CBHW041625140626
46547CB00030B/967